M'Liss Rae Hawley's

fat quarter quilts

FABRIC CHOICES, EASY PIECING & QUILTING IDEAS

C&T PUBLISHING

Text © 2007 M'Liss Rae Hawley

Artwork © 2007 C&T Publishing, Inc.

Publisher: *Amy Marson*

Editorial Director: *Gailen Runge*

Acquisitions Editor: *Jan Grigsby*

Editor: *Darra Williamson*

Technical Editors: *Teresa Stroin and Nanette S. Zeller*

Copyeditor/Proofreader: *Wordfirm Inc.*

Cover Designer: *Christina D. Jarumay*

Design Director/Book Designer: *Rose Sheifer-Wright*

Illustrator: *John Heisch*

Production Coordinator: *Zinnia Heinzmann*

Photography: *Luke Mulks, Diane Pedersen*, and *Sharon Risedorph*, unless otherwise noted. Author photo by *Michael Stadler*.

Published by C&T Publishing, Inc., P.O. Box 1456, Lafayette, CA 94549

Front cover: *The Square—Copenhagen* (background), *A Path Less Traveled, Deputy Sheriff,* and *Window of Opportunity* by **M'Liss Rae Hawley**

Back cover: *Framed in Starlight* by **M'Liss Rae Hawley**

Library of Congress Cataloging-in-Publication Data

Hawley, M'Liss Rae.
  M'Liss Rae Hawley's fat quarter quilts : Fabric choices, easy piecing & quilting ideas
/ M'Liss Rae Hawley.
    p. cm.
  ISBN-13: 978-1-57120-404-2 (paper trade : alk. paper)
  ISBN-10: 1-57120-404-0 (paper trade : alk. paper)
  1. Patchwork--Patterns. 2. Quilting--Patterns. I. Title.

TT835.H347125 2007
746.46'041--dc22
                                    2006026068

Printed in China
10 9 8 7 6 5 4 3 2 1

CONTENTS

Dedication

To my parents, Josephine Walsh and Kenneth Ray Frandsen,
I lovingly dedicate this book.

Acknowledgments

I would like to thank—both personally and professionally—
the following people and companies, who share my vision,
enthusiasm, and love of quilting, and to express my gratitude for
their contributions to the industry.

C&T Publishing: Amy Marson, Jan Grigsby, Darra Williamson,
Teresa Stroin, Christina D. Jarumay, Rose Sheifer-Wright,
Zinnia Heinzmann, and all the dedicated staff who continue
to create wonderful books

Husqvarna Viking: Stan Ingraham and Nancy Jewell

Hoffman Fabrics: Sandy Muckenthaler

Quilters Dream Batting: Kathy Thompson

Robison-Anton Textile Company

The Electric Quilt Company: Penny McMorris

Peggy Johnson, the Keeper of the Blocks, who helped draft the
patterns in the book with The Electric Quilt Company software

Friends Vicki, Peggy, Susie, and John and my sister, Erin, for the
last-minute help with piecing and bindings

Tony Kowal, for continuing to be a source of inspiration and
support, as well as a wonderful friend

A special thank-you to my amazing contributors, who worked
with me on this, my fourth book on fat-quarter quilts, at Useless
Bay Golf and Country Club on Whidbey Island, Washington. They
are a dedicated and talented group of quilters, and they continue to
inspire me in many ways

Finally, thank you to Michael, Adrienne, and Alexander—
my family.

Introduction

Welcome back to the magical world of fat-quarter quilts! Fat quarters are more addictive than chocolate. They are the quick-fix snack for fabriholics, and we just can't seem to resist.

Fat quarters sit in a place of honor in fabric stores—beautiful, coordinated packets tied together with ribbon. We're tempted by boxes and baskets overflowing with these luscious treats.

It's easy to be overwhelmed by the sheer number of choices as you begin a new quilt. *Fat Quarter Quilts* reduces your variables and guarantees success. Pick a pattern, grab your fat quarters, and join me on a wonderful adventure!

Fat quarters are more addictive than chocolate.

Fat-Quarter-Friendly Fabric and Tools

Working with fat quarters doesn't mean you have to make only small-scale quilts. The size of the fat quarter dictates the size of the blocks or units, not the overall size of the quilt. Full size, queen size, even king size—the sky's the limit!

The patterns in the book call for six or more fat quarters to use for the primary design or motif (Framed in Starlight on page 42 uses nineteen!), background fabric (fat quarters of multiple fabrics or a single piece of fabric), and yardage for borders, bindings, and backing. We'll start with the fat quarters—naturally!

What *Is* a Fat Quarter?

Unlike a standard $1/4$ yard of fabric, which is cut across the full width of the fabric and measures $9'' \times 42''$, a fat quarter is $1/2$ yard of fabric ($18'' \times 42''$)

Deputy Sheriff, my version of Pony Express Star (page 63), uses six fat quarters for the block centers, a single light background fabric, and various fabrics for star points, setting elements, borders, and binding.

A standard $1/4$ yard (cut from the bolt) versus a fat quarter

cut in half along the lengthwise grain of the fabric. A fat quarter should measure $18'' \times 21''$.

In reality, when you examine fat-quarter pieces, you may notice slight differences in size, even within the same packet of fabrics. This variation can happen for a number of reasons. Some manufacturers' fabrics are slightly narrower than the industry standard of $42''$. Some shops consistently cut their fat quarters slightly larger or smaller. Selvages may reduce the usable dimensions.

What happens after you bring your fabric home can also make a difference in the size of your fat quarters. Prewashing, a practice I advocate, can shrink fabric slightly, and the washing machine has a tendency to fray smaller pieces of fabric even more than it does larger ones.

Because of these variables, I've based the patterns in this book on fat quarters that measure $17\frac{1}{2}'' \times 20''$ after laundering. I suggest that you measure all your fat quarters after you wash them. Measuring can spare you surprises (and frustration) when you begin cutting. Depending on the usable size of your fat quarters, you may want or need to add additional fat quarters. You may decide to make more or fewer blocks than the instructions call for.

As you look at the photos in this book, you'll see quilts of different sizes made from the same pattern. In some cases, the quilters simply—and creatively—made do.

I prewash all new fabrics—fat quarters in the sink, 1/2-yard and larger pieces in the washing machine—and dry them in the dryer. As soon as they come from the dryer, the fabrics are ironed (by my husband, Michael), squared up (with the help of our daughter, Adrienne), and placed on the shelf in no time.

Working With Fat-Quarter Packets

Whatever level of quilter you are, prepackaged fat-quarter packets are a great place to start in planning your fat-quarter quilt. Look around! Quilt shops, catalogs, and online sources assemble luscious groupings for our convenience—and delight (see Resources on page 78). These handy collections are the ultimate in reducing your variables. Six to eight beautifully coordinating fat quarters make it effortless for the beginner and the experienced quilter alike to assemble the fabrics for a successful quilt.

Here are some suggestions for getting started, depending upon your skill level. Once you feel comfortable, push yourself to the next level.

- Beginners: Go to your favorite quilt shop, catalog, or website and purchase your favorite packet.

- Confident beginners: Do the same, but buy fabric that appears to be a challenge for you.

- Intermediate-level quilters: Buy two coordinating packets of six fat quarters and mix them up.

- Totally confident quilters: Get really creative! Mix fat quarters from packets with fat quarters already in your stash, or build your own fat-quarter packets.

Creating Your Own Fat-Quarter Packet

With so many new fabrics appearing each season, you might find that your favorite quilt shop or other fabric resource doesn't have the perfect fat-quarter packet to re-create the look you want for a particular quilt. Perhaps you want the challenge of building your own fat-quarter packet to make one of the quilts in this book. Where do you begin?

When I'm not buying precut or prepackaged fat quarters, I typically purchase a minimum of 5/8 yard off the bolt. This yardage gives me two fat quarters (one to share with a friend perhaps) plus a little extra. When I'm choosing fabric for a border, I buy the necessary yardage plus an additional 1/2 yard, in case I wish to include this fabric as a fat quarter too.

A fabric collection is a great way to go about building your own fat-quarter packet and to select coordinating border and background fabrics for a quilt. The prints in a collection are designed to harmonize, the colorways are coordinated, and the ultimate look is very together.

I often suggest to my students that they select the pattern first; the pattern may bring a specific fabric or theme to mind. Alternative sources of inspiration include the following:

- A theme: A holiday, season, or special event can often direct your choice of fabric.

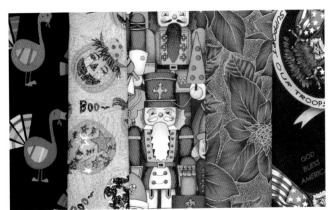
Examples of holiday, seasonal, and special event fabrics

- A background or border fabric: A dark background may dictate different fat-quarter selections than does a light background. If you see a potential border fabric that captures your imagination—whether in the quilt shop or already in your stash—this may be the place to start.

Background and border fabrics can inspire other fabric choices.

■ A color: Do you have a favorite color? One that you consider a challenge? A color you've never worked with but are anxious to try? Use this color—in all its variations—as your inspiration.

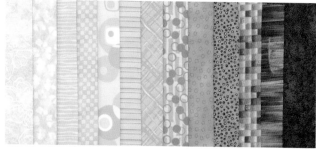

A color—in all its variations and values—can be a great jumping-off point.

Once you have a starting point, you are ready to choose the fat quarters to make up your own personal packet. As a rule, a variety of prints (pattern and scale), colors, and values (lights, mediums, and darks) will make your quilt more interesting.

I like to mix it up. I'll choose a plaid, a small-scale blender fabric, a larger-scale print, a subtle tone-on-tone print, and perhaps a print that continues the theme. Stripes are always fun! Don't forget to add a zinger: a fabric that adds a touch of the main color's complement or picks up an unusual color in the theme fabric. You don't have to love every fabric in your fat-quarter assortment. A mixture of textures, layers of color, and a bold departure from your comfort zone make for a great fat-quarter quilt.

Aim for a variety of prints (pattern and scale) and values in your fat-quarter packet.

Value, which refers to the lightness or darkness of a color in relationship to those around it, is an essential factor in the success of your quilt. Value creates contrast and allows you to see the pattern emerge. Even if you make a one-color (monochromatic) quilt, the range of values within that single color is what makes the quilt work.

Choosing Background Fabric

How important is the background fabric? It is as significant as your fat quarters! The background fabric may represent up to half of the pieced quilt. Choosing a background fabric may not be the first decision you make, but then again you may have a wonderful piece of background fabric you want to build your quilt around.

Each pattern in this book uses a single background fabric, but there is no reason you can't use more than one. Let the style, proportion, and dimensions of the block or pattern guide you in determining the number of background fabrics. Personally, I love the look of multiple backgrounds. The variety adds depth, texture, and visual interest. A small, simple block made from just a few pieces is a good candidate for multiple background fabrics. The contrast in visual textures (prints) and the slight variations in value (lights and darks) all add to the richness of the design.

On the other hand, for a pattern composed of lots of pieces and many units, such as Pony Express Star, the introduction of multiple background fabrics might prove downright distracting.

The addition of multiple background fabrics could easily overwhelm the eye in the visually complex Pony Express Star pattern.

Background fabrics are often relatively light in value, creating a nice contrast with foreground fat-quarter fabrics. Of course, this is not an absolute!

Carla Zimmermann used a very dark (black) background fabric for the triangles in *Pretty Maids All in a Row* (page 31), her version of the simple Danish Square pattern. The dark background makes the vividly colored prints even more intense.

Assess your fat-quarter assortment. Depending upon what you see, you may prefer to go darker for your background. The result isn't wrong—it's just different.

Quilters often choose neutral colors for backgrounds. Technically, neutral means free from color (examples of neutral colors are white, gray, and black), but I like to think that quilters can take liberties and add their own personal neutral colors to the standard list. Your neutral may simply be your favorite color in its lightest value.

I have three colors that I personally consider my neutrals: yellow, green, and pink. I used one of these favorites—yellow—as the background for *The Square—Copenhagen* (page 27). When I find fabrics in a light version of any of these colors, they go straight to the cutting counter. Fabric colors are seasonal and regional; buy what you like when you see it.

As always, you can take your cue from the theme fabric. Is the lightest value white or beige? Does the theme fabric lend itself to a colored background—your personal neutral? Finding the right background fabric or fabrics for your fat-quarter quilt is just another step in a wonderful journey. Take time in making choices now. The end results will be well worth it.

I used yellow as a neutral background in my interpretation of the Danish Square pattern.

Choosing Border Fabrics

Some of the patterns in this book, such as Parallel Paths (page 57) and Framed in Starlight (page 42), do not include traditional inner and outer borders. Other patterns, such as Showcase (page 72) and

Crossings (page 21), include a narrow inner border between the center quilt design and the outer, wider border. Either way, you'll want to choose border fabrics that complement and enhance your design, rather than overpower it.

Many prepackaged fat-quarter packets are cut from fabrics that have just arrived at your local quilt shop. As a result, the fabrics in the packet are usually still available on the bolt. Repeating one of the fat quarters as your border fabric is a can't-miss method for finishing your quilt.

Large-scale prints make great outer borders for fat-quarter quilts—as you can see from many of the quilts in this book! You'll need to plan ahead though. Some large-scale prints are pictorial, directional, or both, so they may require extra yardage, as well as extra time and effort in the planning and cutting.

Examples of large-scale directional border fabrics

There are many other options for selecting an appropriate border fabric:

- Misunderstood, overlooked, and often under-used, striped fabrics make fabulous borders. Check out *Persian Prayer Rug* (page 32) and see for yourself!

- If your quilt features a wide range of prints, colors, or both, a multicolored paisley or floral can tie them together. My quilt *A Place to Ponder* (page 50) and Anastasia Riordan's *Invitation Into Gold* (page 26) are good examples.

- *Chicago Jazz Scene* (page 76) and *Pony Espresso* (page 71) demonstrate the success of a border fabric chosen to reflect the quilt's theme.

Now that you've gotten started, no doubt you'll come up with many of your own creative solutions.

Choosing Binding Fabric

Usually the binding is the darkest fabric in the quilt, or it repeats the fabric in the outer border. I like to continue the motif or theme of the outer border in my choice of binding fabric. If, for instance, I use a floral print in the outer border, I'll use the same floral print or another, similar floral print as the binding.

Working With Fat Quarters

Once I have the idea for a block (or quilt) on paper, I actually make a sample block in scrap fabric. Sometimes I hit it absolutely right the first time. Sometimes a little adjustment does the trick. Often, all I need to do is simplify the design a bit— for example, by eliminating a seam or a shape. Sometimes I just need to make the block a bit smaller to get the necessary yield from my fat-quarter pieces. Re-creating the block in fabric helps me to visualize the possibilities.

Don't be afraid to look beyond the boundaries of a square block. You can stretch your block into a rectangle, as I did with Danish Square (page 27). You can even eliminate the confines of the block completely: make the entire quilt top your design and build it from simple shapes and units. Parallel Paths (page 57) and Garden Gate (page 50) are good examples of patterns without blocks.

Sometimes an idea does not work out as originally planned and instead, given a bit of time and patience, evolves into something entirely different— and often better. This happens to me often enough that I've learned to trust my instincts and not give up too quickly. Some of my best designs have happened this way!

Gathering the Equipment

One of the best things about fat-quarter quilts is that you don't need a lot of fancy gadgets or special equipment to make them. The basics, including typical rotary-cutting supplies, work perfectly. Here is a list of what you'll need, with thoughts about my favorite features:

Rotary cutter: with an ergonomic-style grip, reliable safety catch, and a new blade.

Cutting mat: green, with a grid. Lines indicating 45° angles are helpful.

Acrylic rulers: both 6″ × 24″ and 6″ × 12″ sizes, preferably with 45° angles indicated.

Ruler grips: the clear type. These adhesive tabs stick to the bottom of your rulers to keep them from slipping as you cut.

Pins: fine, glass-head silk pins. They don't leave unsightly holes in the fabric.

Scissors: both fabric scissors and small embroidery-type scissors for cutting thread.

Seam ripper: with an ergonomic-style handle.

Thread: 100% cotton thread in a neutral color for piecing.

Sewing machine needles: Keep a good supply on hand to change after each project.

Sewing machine: in good working order, with a ¼″ presser foot to help keep your piecing accurate. If your machine did not come with this foot, I strongly recommend that you buy one!

Additional attachments: A dual-feed, or walking, foot is a must for straight-line quilting and for applying binding by machine. An open-toe stippling foot (also called a darning foot) is useful for free-motion quilting. For attaching trims, as on the border of Crossings (page 21), a cording or braiding foot makes the job go much more smoothly.

The fat-quarter quilts in this book are generally easy to make. I've streamlined the instructions to take advantage of the various rotary-cutting and quick-piecing techniques we quiltmakers have come to know and rely on.

Rotary Cutting

The process for rotary cutting fat quarters is pretty much the same as for cutting yardage, except the fabric pieces are smaller. The following guidelines work for both.

Squaring Your Fabric

Square the edges of your fabrics before rotary cutting them into strips and smaller pieces. Squaring is especially important with fat quarters. The pieces of fabric are small, and every inch is precious. The instructions for each project tell you which edge of the fat quarter to cut.

Press the fabric and fold it carefully before you begin. You need to fold a fat quarter only once. Fold larger pieces twice or break them down so that you can work with a more manageable amount.

1. Place the folded fabric on the cutting mat with the fold closest to you.

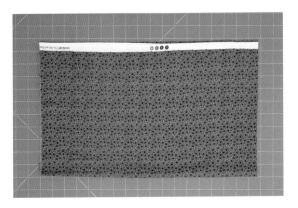

2. Position your ruler on the right-hand edge of the fabric so that the ruler is perpendicular to the fold. Trim a narrow strip from the right-hand edge of the fabric to square it up.

3. Rotate the fabric (or the mat) 180° and repeat Step 2 at the opposite edge.

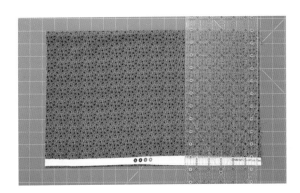

Cutting Strips and Pieces

Whether you are cutting fat quarters or yardage, use the lines on your ruler, not on your mat, to measure and cut the strips and pieces. Use the mat grid only for aligning the fabric and taking rough measurements.

1. Working from the squared left edge of the fabric, measure and cut a strip of the desired width. Repeat to cut the required number of strips. You may need to square up the end after every few cuts.

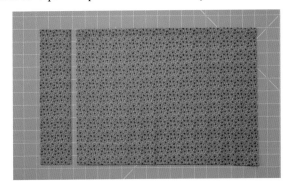

2. Cut the strips into squares or other smaller segments as directed in the project instructions.

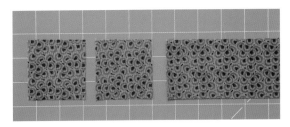

Piecing and Pressing

Unless noted otherwise, use a ¼″ seam allowance for piecing the quilts in this book. It's always a good idea to check that your ¼″ seam is accurate before beginning to sew.

For projects made from blocks, you'll sew pieces into units, units into rows, and rows together to complete the blocks. I will tell you which way to press the seams, either in the instructions themselves or with arrows in the accompanying diagrams.

Press lightly with a lifting-and-lowering motion. Dragging the iron across the fabric can distort the individual pieces and the finished blocks.

Assembling the Quilt

Some patterns in this book—for example Showcase (page 72) and Framed by Starlight (page 42)—are sewn together in the straight set. The blocks are arranged in horizontal rows, with the block edges parallel to the sides of the quilt. The blocks are sewn together with ¼″ seam

allowances to create the rows, and the seams are pressed in opposite directions from row to row. Then the rows are sewn together, and the seams are pressed, usually in one direction.

Straight set

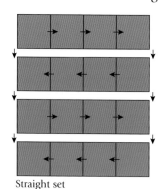

Tips for Machine Embroidery

The Embroidered Windows pattern (page 33) includes blocks that feature machine embroidery. Other patterns, such as Garden Gate (page 50), suggest optional machine-embroidered cornerstones. These are just a few ideas for introducing the beauty of machine embroidery to your quilts. I'm sure you'll think of many others.

- Prewash the fabric you plan to use as background for the embroidery designs. Washing will preshrink the fabric, which is a necessary step.
- Begin your embroidery with a new needle and change it during the process if the point becomes dull. Skipped stitches are one indication of a dull needle. Some embroidery designs have more than 10,000 stitches. A dull needle can distort the design.
  - Outfit your machine with an embroidery foot.
  - Prewind several bobbins with polyester, rayon, or cotton bobbin-fill thread, such as Robison-Anton filament polyester bobbin thread. Or purchase prewound bobbins such as those manufactured by Robison-Anton. Choose white or black, using the background fabric as your guide; or you may want to change the bobbin thread as the color of the top thread changes.

The blocks in Crossings (page 21) are arranged in a traditional diagonal, or on-point, set. In this set, the blocks are arranged in diagonal rows, with the block edges at a 45° angle to the sides of the quilt. The zigzag edges are filled in with half- and quarter-square triangles to straighten the edges of the quilt top. (The project instructions tell you how many of these triangles to cut and how big to cut them.) The blocks and side triangles are sewn together with

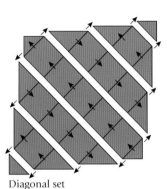

¼″ seam allowances to create the diagonal rows, with the seams pressed in opposite directions from row to row. The corner triangles are added next, and finally the rows are sewn together and pressed.

Diagonal set

Parallel Paths (page 57) is an example of the traditional coins set. The quilt is assembled in rows instead of blocks, and then the rows are sewn together, often with strips of sashing between the rows and with seams pressed toward the sashing strips.

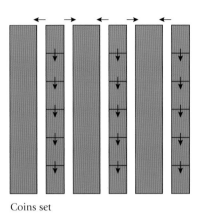

Coins set

- Select a fabric stabilizer to use under the background fabric. There are many types of stabilizers available—my favorite is a midweight tear-away product manufactured by Sulky (see Resources on page 78). Whichever you choose, read the manufacturer's instructions *carefully*. Some stabilizers are heat- or water-sensitive. I prefer a tear-away stabilizer when I machine embroider on 100% cotton fabric. Sometimes a liquid stabilizer works well with a lightweight or light-colored fabric. If the fabric is prone to puckering, try a water-soluble or heat-sensitive stabilizer.
- An embroidery hoop is key; it keeps the fabric from shifting as you embroider the designs. If possible, place the fabric in the hoop so that it is straight on the grain. Avoid puckers and pleats. The fabric should be pulled taut but not too tight.
- Stitch a test of the desired embroidery design, using the fabric, threads, and stabilizer you plan to use for the project. You'll be able to tell whether the thread tension is correct, whether the thread coverage is sufficient, and whether the embroidered design will look good on the background fabric you've chosen so you can make any necessary adjustments. If you wish, you can incorporate your test design into your label or quilt backing.

Adding Borders

The quilts in this book include three different border treatments: squared borders, borders with cornerstones, and mitered borders. Framed in Starlight (page 42) is the exception. Shooting Star blocks create the illusion of a border surrounding the Log Cabin center.

Squared Borders

1. Measure the finished quilt top through the center from side to side. Cut 2 borders to this measurement for top and bottom borders.

2. Place pins at the center of the top and bottom of the quilt top, as well as at the midpoint of each border strip. Pin the borders to the quilt top, matching the ends and center points. Use additional pins as needed, easing or gently stretching the border to fit. Sew the borders to the quilt top with a ¹⁄₄″ seam allowance. Press as instructed—usually toward the borders.

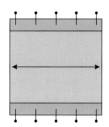

3. Measure the quilt from top to bottom, including the borders you've just sewn. Cut 2 borders to this measurement for the side borders. Repeat Step 2 to pin, sew, and press the borders.

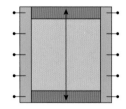

Borders With Cornerstones

The instructions for Garden Gate (page 50) include borders with cornerstones. Some of the other quilts include this option as well.

1. Measure the quilt top through the center from side to side and from top to bottom. Cut 2 borders to each of these measurements.

2. Sew the appropriately sized strips to the top and bottom of the quilt. Press the seams toward the borders. Sew a cornerstone to each end of the remaining borders. Press the seams toward the borders. Sew the border units to the sides of the quilt and press the seams toward the borders.

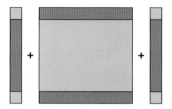

Mitered Borders

1. Measure the finished quilt top through the center from top to bottom to find the length of the quilt. To this measurement, add 2 times the width of the border, plus 5″. Cut 2 borders to this measurement for the *side* borders. Measure the finished quilt top from side to side to find the width of the quilt. To this measurement, add 2 times the width of the border, plus 5″. Cut 2 borders to this measurement for the *top and bottom* borders.

2. Place pins to mark the centers of all sides of the quilt top, as well as the midpoint of each border strip.

3. Measure and pin-mark *half the length* of the quilt top on both sides of the center pin on each side border strip. Pin the borders to the sides of the quilt, matching the pins at the midpoints and the pins marking the quilt length to the edges of the quilt top. (The excess border length will extend beyond each edge of the quilt.)

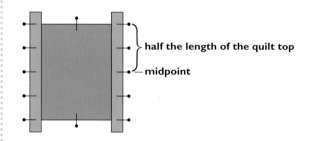

half the length of the quilt top

midpoint

4. Stitch the border to the sides of the quilt, stopping ¼″ from the edge of the quilt with a backstitch. Press the seams toward the borders.

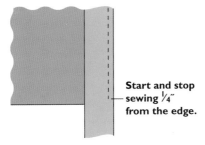

Start and stop sewing ¼″ from the edge.

5. Measure and pin-mark *half the width* of the quilt top on both sides of the center pin on the top and bottom border strips. Pin the borders to the top and bottom of the quilt, matching the pins at the center points and the pins marking the quilt width to the edges of the quilt. (Again, the excess border length will extend beyond each edge of the quilt.) Repeat Step 4 to sew the top and bottom borders to the quilt.

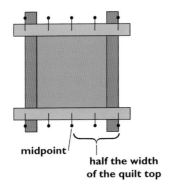

midpoint

half the width of the quilt top

6. To create the miter, place a corner of the quilt right side up on your ironing board. Place the excess tail of one of the border strips on top of the adjacent border strip.

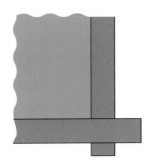

7. Fold the top border strip under at a 45° angle so that it meets the edge of the bottom border strip. Press lightly. Use a ruler or right-angle triangle to be certain that the angle is correct and that the corner is square. Press the fold again, firmly this time.

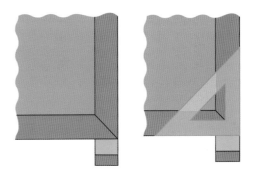

8. Fold the quilt top diagonally, right sides together, and align the long edges of the border strips. Place pins near the pressed fold to secure the corners for sewing.

9. Beginning with a backstitch at the inside corner of the border, carefully stitch toward the outside edge along the fold. Finish with a backstitch.

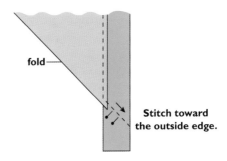

fold

Stitch toward the outside edge.

10. Trim the seam allowance to ¼″ and press the seam open.

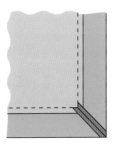

Preparing Your Quilt for Quilting

Don't skimp in preparing your quilt for quilting! Take the time to layer it properly and baste it sufficiently.

Batting and Backing

The choice of batting is a personal decision, but you'll want to consider the method (and amount) of quilting you plan to do, as well as the quilt's end use.

Cut the batting and the backing approximately 4˝ larger than the quilt top on all sides. You'll sometimes need to piece the fabric to have a large enough backing piece. The yardage specified in the projects is enough for vertical seams. Prewash the backing fabric and remove the selvages first.

Layering and Basting

Unlike many machine quilters, I prefer to hand baste with thread rather than pin baste.

1. Carefully press the quilt top from the back to set the seams and then press from the front. Press the backing. If you wish, use spray starch or sizing.

2. Spread the backing wrong side up and secure it with masking tape. The fabric should be taut but not stretched. Center the batting over the backing. Finally, center the quilt top right side up over the batting.

3. Thread a long needle with light-colored thread. Beginning in the center of the quilt, stitch a 4˝ grid of horizontal and vertical lines.

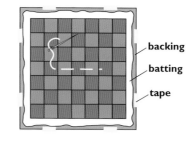

backing

batting

tape

4. Remove the tape and get ready to quilt.

Quilting Your Quilt

A quilt becomes a quilt when it includes three layers—a top, a layer of batting, and a backing—all secured with stitching of some type to hold the layers together. (This means that to call your project a quilt, you need to finish it!) Some quilters create that stitching by hand; others, by machine. My quilts in this book—as well as almost all the quilts made by my wonderful group of quilters—were machine quilted.

Each step of the quiltmaking process, including the machine quilting, is exciting and fun to me. I love the idea of adding yet another level of creativity to my quilts. Machine quilting my own tops gives me flexibility in making those design decisions, and I do my own quilting whenever I can. Because of time constraints, however, I find I must now have many of my quilt tops professionally machine quilted. If you have stacks of quilt tops waiting to be quilted, you might want to consider that option.

Machine quilting is an art form, so there is a learning curve involved. Practice is the best way to learn and master this skill. Here are some guidelines to get you started.

Dual-Feed Foot

The dual-feed foot is designed to hold and feed the three layers of your quilt evenly as you stitch. Use this foot to machine quilt single lines or parallel lines and grids—whether vertical, horizontal, or diagonal. You can also use this foot for certain decorative stitches and embellishing techniques, such as couching.

Dual-feed foot

Open-Toe Stippling Foot

Also called a darning foot, the open-toe stippling foot allows you to quilt in all directions: you are the guide! Use this foot for stipple quilting, meandering, and other free-motion techniques. I like to stipple quilt around machine-embroidered motifs, because this causes the embroidered design to pop out and become a focal point.

Open-toe stippling foot

You will need to drop the feed dogs on your sewing machine when you use the open-toe stippling foot. You might also need to set the presser foot pressure to the darning position so you can move the quilt at a smooth pace for consistent stitches. Some machines have a built-in stipple stitch, which is a wonderful way to achieve this beautiful surface texture.

Threads

I consider quilting thread to be a design element, not just the means to hold the three layers of my quilts together. I also believe that variety in thread adds visual interest and showcases the quilter's individuality. For these reasons, I frequently use a mix of threads in my quilts. When choosing thread, I consider thread color, texture, and weight as well as where I plan to use the thread.

Typical thread choices for machine quilting include rayon (35- and 40-weight), cotton, polyester, and monofilament. I use lots of variegated and metallic threads, as well as novelty threads, such as Twister Tweeds, Swirling Sensation, and Moon Glow (see Resources on page 78).

I use a wide variety of threads in my quilts.

Design

Let your imagination be your guide in choosing quilting motifs for your fat-quarter quilts. Design sources are everywhere! Look carefully at quilts in museums, shows, books, and magazines; at books of quilting patterns; and at quilting stencils. Observe patterns in other areas of your life—particularly patterns in nature.

Begin by anchoring key seams in and around blocks and borders by stitching in the ditch along the seamlines. Try filling in open spaces with loops, curves, clamshells, and waves. Combine straight and curvy lines for variety.

I love to use heavy free-motion quilting, such as stippling, in the backgrounds behind pieced, appliquéd, and embroidered motifs. Heavy quilting causes the background to recede and the motif to pop forward, taking center stage in the design.

Note how the heavily quilted background in the blocks of *Window of Opportunity* (page 33) makes the embroideries seem to pop.

One of my favorite options is to let the fabric inspire me. I can stitch a garden trellis over a floral fabric or add detail to a beach with quilted rocks and shells. I also love to pull a motif from the fabric and adapt it for quilting in another area of the quilt. A simpler option is to follow the fabric motif right where it is. The latter option is especially effective in a large-scale background fabric or outer-border fabric.

To get you started, I've included an illustration with each of the project quilts showing the quilting motifs that Barbara Dau and I collaborated to create.

I chose the black-and-white fabric in the Showcase blocks as inspiration for the border quilting in my quilt *Harlequin Carnival* (page 72).

Finishing Your Quilt

The binding, hanging sleeve, and label of your quilt are important too, so be sure to give them the same attention you've given to every other element.

Squaring Up

Before adding the binding, you need to trim the excess batting and backing and square up your quilt. Use the seams of the outer borders as a guide.

1. Align a ruler with the outer-border seam and measure to the edge of the quilt in several places. Use the narrowest measurement as a guide for positioning your ruler and trim the excess batting and backing all around the quilt.

2. Fold the quilt in half lengthwise and crosswise to check that the corners are square and that the sides are equal in length. If they aren't, use a large square ruler to even them up, one corner at a time.

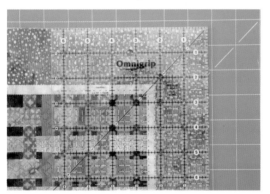

3. Stabilize the quilt edges by stitching around the perimeter with a basting or serpentine stitch. (Do not use a zigzag stitch—it can push and pull the fabric out of shape.)

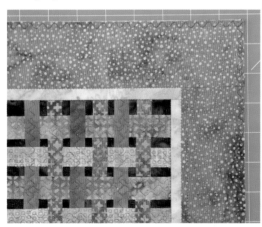

4. Remove any stray threads or bits of batting from the quilt top. You are now ready to bind your quilt.

Making and Applying Binding

Binding is an important and, sadly, often overlooked step in the quiltmaking process. Many a wonderful quilt is spoiled by a poorly sewn binding. Take your time deciding what fabric you will use and enjoy the process of stitching it to your quilt. You're coming down the home stretch now!

Typically, I cut binding strips 3″ wide from selvage to selvage across the width of the fabric. I make an exception and cut strips on the bias only when I want to create a special effect with a plaid or striped fabric or when I need to follow a curved or rounded edge.

The following method is the one I use to bind my quilts. It results in a finished edge that is attractive and strong.

1. Cut enough binding strips to go around the perimeter (outside edges) of the quilt, plus an extra 10″ for seams and corners. Sew the strips together at right angles, as shown. Trim the excess fabric from the seams, leaving a ¼″ seam allowance, and press the seams open.

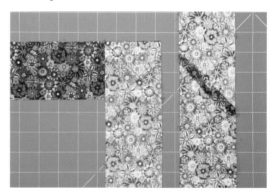

2. Fold the binding in half lengthwise, wrong sides together, and press.

3. Starting 6″ down from the upper right corner and with the raw edges even, place the binding on the quilt top. Check to see that none of the diagonal seams falls on a corner of the quilt. If one does, adjust the starting point. Begin stitching 4″ from the end of the binding, using a ¹/₂″ seam allowance.

4. Stitch about 2″ and then stop and cut the threads. Remove the quilt from the machine and fold the binding to the back of the quilt. The binding should cover the line of machine stitching on the back. If the binding overlaps the stitching too much, try again, taking a slightly wider seam allowance. If the binding doesn't cover the original line of stitching, take a slightly narrower seam allowance. Remove the unwanted stitches before you continue.

5. Using the stitching position you determined in Step 4, resume stitching until you are ¹/₂″ from the first corner of the quilt. Stop, backstitch, cut the thread, and remove the quilt from the machine.

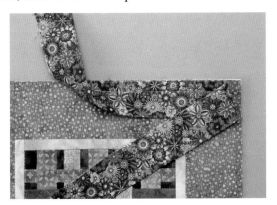

6. Fold the binding to create a mitered corner.

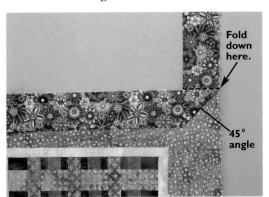

Fold down here.

45° angle

7. Resume stitching, mitering each corner as you come to it.

8. Stop stitching about 3″ after you've turned the last corner. Make sure the starting and finishing ends of the binding overlap by at least 4″. Cut the threads and remove the quilt from the machine. Measure a 3″ overlap and trim the excess binding.

9. Place the quilt right side up. Unfold the unstitched binding tails, place them right sides together at right angles, and pin them together. Draw a line from the upper left corner to the lower right corner of the binding and stitch on the drawn line.

10. Carefully trim the seam allowance to ¹/₄″ and press the seam open. Refold the binding and press. Finish stitching the binding to the quilt.

11. Turn the binding to the back of the quilt and pin it. (I pin approximately 12″ at a time.) Use matching-colored thread to blindstitch the binding to the quilt back, carefully mitering the corners as you approach them. Hand stitch the miters on both sides.

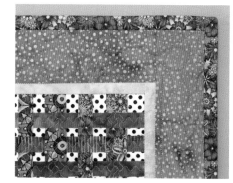

Making and Adding a Sleeve

If you want to display your quilt on a wall, you need to add a sleeve to protect your work of art from excessive strain.

1. Cut an 8½″-wide strip of backing fabric 1″ shorter than the width of the quilt. (If the quilt is wider than 40″, cut 2 strips and stitch them together end to end.) Fold under the short ends ¼″; stitch and press.

2. Fold the sleeve in half lengthwise, right sides together. Sew the long raw edges together and press the seam open. Turn the sleeve right side out and press again.

3. Mark the midpoint of the sleeve and the top edge of the quilt. Match the midpoints and pin the sleeve to the quilt with the seam on the sleeve at the top edge, right below the binding. Use matching-colored thread to blindstitch the top edge in place.

4. Push up the bottom edge of the sleeve ¼″ so that when the hanging rod is inserted, it will not put strain on the quilt. Blindstitch the bottom edge of the sleeve, taking care not to catch the front of the quilt as you stitch.

Creating a Label

I always recommend making a label for your quilt. A label gives you a place to provide important information about both you and the quilt. I like to make my labels large—about 4″ × 7″—so I have plenty of room. You can sew the label to the lower right corner of the quilt back before it is quilted or wait to attach the label after you have completed the quilt.

I suggest including the following information on your label: the name of the quilt; your full name (and business name, if you have one); your city, county, province or state, and country of residence; and the date.

If the quilt was made for a special person, to commemorate a special event, or as part of a series, you might want to include that information as well. You might also choose to note the name of the quilting teacher who inspired you or to tell a special story connected to the quilt.

Use the label to record key information about your quilt.

You can make a simple label by drawing and writing on fabric with permanent fabric markers. (Stabilize the fabric first with freezer paper or interfacing.) For a more elaborate (and fun!) label, try photo-transfer techniques, use the lettering system on your sewing machine, or use an embroidery machine to embellish your label. You could even create your own distinctive signature or logo. Include patches, decals, buttons, ribbons, or lace. I often include leftover blocks to tie the quilt top to the back.

Crossings

Finished quilt: $60\frac{1}{2}″ \times 71\frac{3}{4}″$
Finished block: $8″ \times 8″$

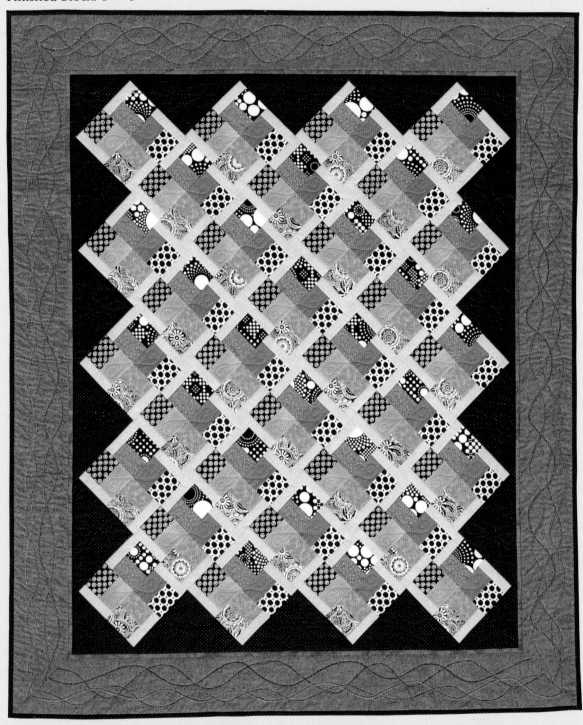

Quirky, But It Works! designed and made by M'Liss Rae Hawley, machine quilted by Barbara Dau, 2006.

I've often been called quirky by my friends. (In checking a thesaurus, I discovered what they *really* are saying is that I'm idiosyncratic, peculiar, and eccentric!) My life embraces many crossings, including the countless ferryboat sailings unique to life on the island where I live, as well as the more typical passages of graduation and marriage—or simply the journey to a quilt shop to purchase fabric for the next project. *Quirky, But It Works!* is just another expression of my colorful personality and the many crossings in my life.

Materials

Fat quarters require 17½″ × 20″ of usable fabric. All other yardages are based on 40″-wide fabric.

- Fat quarters of 4 assorted medium to dark fabrics for blocks
- Fat quarters of 4 assorted light fabrics for blocks
- ¾ yard of fabric for sashing
- 1⅛ yards of fabric for setting triangles
- ⅓ yard of fabric for inner border
- 1½ yards of fabric for outer border
- ¾ yard of fabric for binding
- ½ yard of fabric for hanging sleeve
- 4¾ yards of fabric for backing
- 68″ × 79″ piece of batting
- Decorative yarn, trims, and ribbon (optional)

Cutting

Cut along the 17½″ length of the fat quarters. For the remaining fabrics, cut strips on the crosswise grain (from selvage to selvage).

From *each* (light, medium, and dark) fat quarter:
Cut 7 strips, 2½″ × 17½″.

From the sashing fabric:
Cut 16 strips, 1½″ × 40″; crosscut into 128 rectangles, 1½″ × 4½″.

From the setting-triangle fabric:
Cut 4 squares, 14″ × 14″. Cut each square twice diagonally to make 16 quarter-square, side setting triangles.
Cut 2 squares, 8″ × 8″. Cut each square once diagonally to make 4 half-square, corner setting triangles.

From the inner-border fabric:
Cut 8 strips, 1⅛″ × 40″.

From the outer-border fabric:
Cut 8 strips, 6½″ × 40″.

From the binding fabric:
Cut 8 strips, 3″ × 40″.

From the hanging-sleeve fabric:
Cut 2 strips, 8½″ × 40″.

Making the Blocks

1. Sort the 2½″-wide fat-quarter strips into pairs of 1 medium or dark fabric and 1 light fabric; you will have 4 fabric pairings. Make 7 matching sets of each pairing for a total of 28 pairs. With right sides together and long edges aligned, stitch each pair of strips together to make a strip set. Press the seam allowances toward the darker fabrics.

Make 28 strip sets in 4 matching sets of 7 pairs each.

2. Crosscut each strip set into four 3½″ fat-quarter segments (112 total). Cut 1 additional segment from 16 strip sets (4 from each fabric pairing). You will have a total of 128 segments.

Cut 128 segments.

3. Sew each fat-quarter segment from Step 2 to a $1^1/2'' \times 4^1/2''$ sashing strip; press. Note that the sashing strip is sewn to the left of the fat-quarter segment and that the lighter fat-quarter fabric is on the top.

4. Arrange 4 different units from Step 3 in 2 rows of 2 units each, as shown. Sew the units into rows; press. Sew the rows together; press. Make 32 blocks.

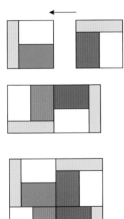

Make 32.

Assembling the Quilt

The side and corner triangles are cut oversized so that the blocks appear to float. You will square up the quilt top after it is assembled.

1. Arrange the blocks and setting triangles in diagonal rows, as shown in the assembly diagram. You will have 2 side setting triangles left over.

2. Sew the blocks together into diagonal rows. Press the seams in alternating directions from row to

row. Add the side setting triangles. Press the seams toward the triangles. (You'll sew the corner setting triangles in the next step.)

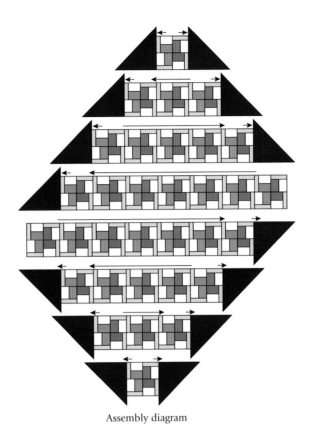

Assembly diagram

3. Sew the rows together; press. Trim the dog ears at each corner, as shown. Sew the corner setting triangles to the quilt. Press the seams toward the triangles.

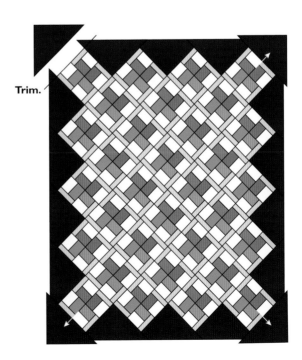

Trim.

4. Square up the quilt top, measuring 1˝ from the points of the blocks to trim the side and corner triangles.

5. With right sides together and long raw edges aligned, sew the 1⅛˝-wide inner-border strips and the 6½˝-wide outer-border strips together in pairs; press. Refer to Mitered Borders (page 14) to measure, fit, and sew the border units to the quilt, piecing as necessary. Miter the corners. Press the seams toward the border units.

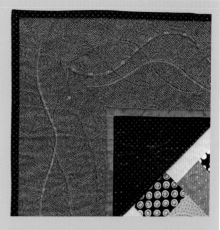

Creative Option

Couch decorative yarn, trims, or ribbon to the border strips before you attach them to the quilt top. Use an erasable marker (I used white chalk) to draw the serpentine design on each individual border strip. Cut a piece of tear-away stabilizer the same size as each border and pin the stabilizer to the back of the marked strip. Use the appropriate sewing machine foot to stitch the desired trim to the quilt.

Finishing the Quilt

Refer to Finishing Your Quilt (page 18).

1. Prepare the backing as described on page 16.

2. Layer the quilt top, batting, and backing; baste.

3. Hand or machine quilt as desired.

4. Use the 3˝-wide strips to bind the edges of the quilt.

5. Add a hanging sleeve and label if desired.

Quilting and embellishing suggestions

Garden Cats,
61″ × 71″, made by Susie Kincy, machine quilted by Barbara Dau, 2006.

Les Poires,
59″ × 69″, made by John and Louise James, machine quilted by Barbara Dau, 2006.

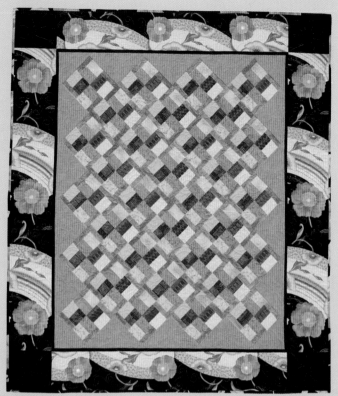

Spicy Salsa, 61″ × 71″, made by Carla Zimmermann, machine quilted by Arlene Anderson, 2006.

Invitation Into Gold, 62″ × 76″, made by Anastasia Riordan, machine quilted by Barbara Dau, 2006.

Autumn's Sunset, 59″ × 70″, made by Annette Barca, machine quilted by Barbara Dau, 2006.

Danish Square

Finished quilt: $39^1/_2'' \times 55^1/_2''$
Finished block: $2'' \times 4''$

The Square—Copenhagen, designed and made by M'Liss Rae Hawley, machine quilted by Barbara Dau, 2006.

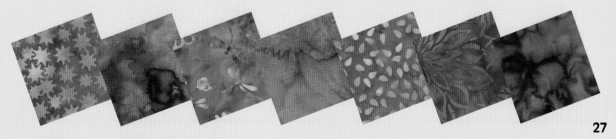

One afternoon last year, while my daughter, Adrienne, and I were in Copenhagen, I looked out our hotel room window onto the old town square. The fading sunset struck the uppermost rooflines of the buildings, reflecting golden sunlight. The view was so beautiful I immediately wanted to capture the image in a quilt.

Just about any fabric palette or theme will work for this quilt. Just be sure to keep contrast in value—lightness and darkness—in mind when you select the background and fat-quarter fabrics.

Materials

Fat quarters require 17½″ × 20″ of usable fabric. All other yardages are based on 40″-wide fabric.

- Fat quarters of 7 assorted fabrics, ranging in value from medium to dark, for blocks
- ⅞ yard of light fabric for blocks
- ¼ yard of fabric for inner border
- 1⅛ yards of fabric for outer border
- ⅝ yard of fabric for binding
- ½ yard of fabric for hanging sleeve
- 3⅝ yards of fabric for backing
- 47″ × 63″ piece of batting

Cutting

Cut along the 20″ length of the fat quarters. For the remaining fabrics, cut strips on the crosswise grain (from selvage to selvage).

From *each* fat quarter:
Cut 6 strips, 2½″ × 20″; crosscut into:
22 rectangles, 2½″ × 4½″ (154 total)
1 square, 2½″ × 2½″ (7 total).

From the light fabric:
Cut 10 strips, 2½″ × 40″; crosscut into 154 squares, 2½″ × 2½″.

From the inner-border fabric:
Cut 6 strips, 1″ × 40″.

From the outer-border fabric:
Cut 6 strips, 5½″ × 40″.

From the binding fabric:
Cut 6 strips, 3″ × 40″.

From the hanging-sleeve fabric:
Cut 2 strips, 8½″ × 40″.

Making the Blocks

1. Use a ruler and marking tool to draw a diagonal line from corner to corner on the wrong side of each 2½″ light square.

2. With right sides together, place a marked 2½″ light square on one end of each 2½″ × 4½″ fat-quarter rectangle, as shown. Sew directly on the marked line. Cut away the excess fabric, leaving a ¼″ seam allowance; press. Make 22 units in each color combination (154 total). Sort and stack matching units in each color combination. Label them blocks 1–7.

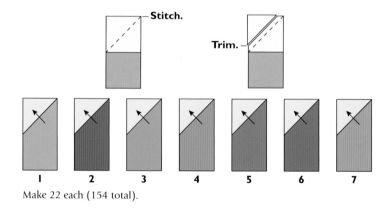

Make 22 each (154 total).

3. Trim 1 of each of blocks 1–7 from Step 2 to make a 2½″ half-block square, as shown. Label these half-blocks 1–7 to match the units from Step 2.

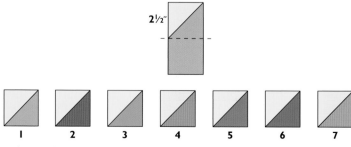

Make 1 each (7 total).

Assembling the Quilt

1. Label the $2\frac{1}{2}''$ medium and dark squares 1–7 to match the blocks and half-blocks.

2. Arrange the blocks, half-blocks, and $2\frac{1}{2}''$ fat-quarter squares in 14 vertical rows, as shown in the assembly diagram below. Note that every other row begins with a $2\frac{1}{2}''$ square and ends with a half-block.

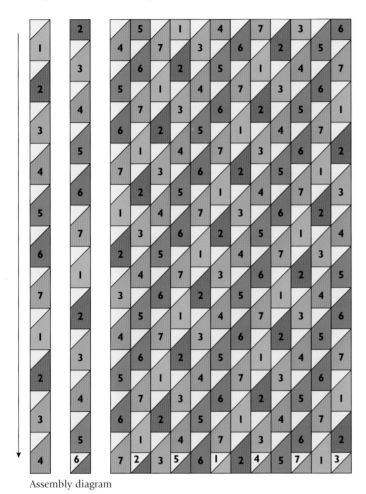

Assembly diagram

3. Beginning in the upper left corner with block 1, sew the blocks, half-blocks, and squares in vertical rows. Press the seams in each row from bottom to top.

4. Sew the rows together, taking care to match the points (see Perfect Points! at right). Press the seams open.

5. With right sides together and long raw edges aligned, sew 1″-wide inner-border strips and $5\frac{1}{2}''$-wide outer-border strips together in pairs; press. Refer to Mitered Borders (page 14) to measure, fit, and sew the border units to the quilt, piecing as necessary. Miter the corners. Press the seams toward the border units.

Perfect Points!

Here's a tip to help you line up the blocks and rows in this quilt with confidence and accuracy.

1. Place the blocks or rows right sides together with seams matching. Insert a vertical placement pin directly through the seam allowances at the exact seam intersection of both pieces. Then place a pin on each side of the place-ment pin.

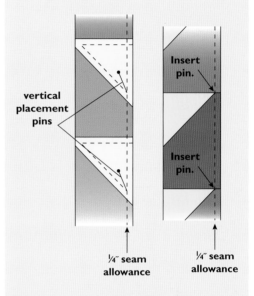

vertical placement pins

Insert pin.

Insert pin.

$\frac{1}{4}''$ seam allowance

$\frac{1}{4}''$ seam allowance

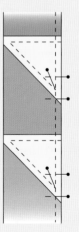

2. Remove the placement pins and stitch.

Finishing the Quilt

Refer to Finishing Your Quilt (page 18).

1. Prepare the backing as described on page 16.
2. Layer the quilt top, batting, and backing; baste.
3. Hand or machine quilt as desired.
4. Use the 3″-wide strips to bind the edges of the quilt.
5. Add a hanging sleeve and label if desired.

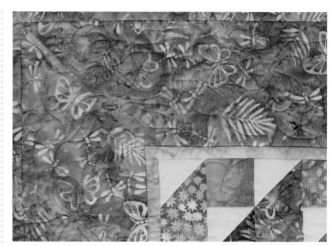

Detail of border quilting

Quilting suggestions

Pretty Maids All in a Row,
40″ × 56″, made by Carla Zimmermann,
machine quilted by Arlene Anderson, 2006.

Climbing Kilimanjaro,
38″ × 54″, made by John and
Louise James, machine quilted
by Kim McKinnon, 2006.

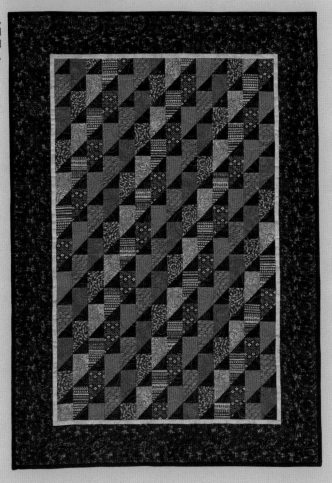

Victorian Flowers,
40″ × 56″, made by Susie
Kincy, machine quilted by
Barbara Dau, 2006.

Persian Prayer Rug,
38″ × 54″, made by
Anastasia Riordan,
machine quilted by
Barbara Dau, 2006.

Embroidered Windows

Finished quilt: $37\frac{1}{2}'' \times 36\frac{1}{4}''$
Finished block: $8'' \times 8''$

Window of Opportunity, designed and made by M'Liss Rae Hawley, machine quilted by Barbara Dau, 2006.

Windows are a recurring theme in my work. My home is filled with windows, and I have numerous areas throughout the house where I enjoy the creative process: an upstairs office, a back porch studio, and a family room with cutting table. All offer different perspectives that vary as the seasons change.

Many of my fabric and embroidery collections reflect these surroundings, and a double Attic Window block makes the perfect vehicle to showcase them. In this quilt, the blocks are offset to give the illusion that the embroideries are floating.

Materials

Fat quarters require $17^1/2" \times 20"$ of usable fabric. All other yardages are based on 40"-wide fabric.

- 1 yard of light fabric for embroidered block centers
- Fat quarter of medium-dark or dark fabric for accent frames
- Fat quarters of 4 assorted fabrics for Attic Window blocks
- Fat quarter of coordinating fabric for filler strips
- Fat quarters of 2 coordinating fabrics for sashing
- $^1/4$ yard of fabric for inner border
- $^3/4$ yard of fabric for outer border
- $^5/8$ yard of fabric for binding
- $^1/2$ yard of fabric for hanging sleeve
- $2^5/8$ yards of fabric for backing
- $45" \times 44"$ piece of batting
- A favorite embroidery collection for embroidered block centers*
- 1 yard of stabilizer for embroideries
    * *You'll need 9 motifs, or you may repeat some.*

Cutting

Cut along the 20" length of the fat quarters. For the remaining fabrics, cut strips on the crosswise grain (from selvage to selvage).

From the light fabric:
  Cut 3 strips, $9^1/2" \times 40"$; crosscut into 9 squares, $9^1/2" \times 9^1/2"$.*
From the accent-frame fat quarter:
  Cut 11 strips, $1" \times 20"$; crosscut into:
    18 rectangles, $1" \times 5"$
    18 rectangles, $1" \times 6"$
From *each* Attic Window fat quarter:
  Cut 5 strips, $1^3/4" \times 20"$ (20 total).
From the filler-strip fat quarter:
  Cut 3 rectangles, $1^3/4" \times 8^1/2"$.
From *each* sashing fat quarter:
  Cut 2 strips, $1^3/4" \times 20"$ (4 total).
From the inner-border fabric:
  Cut 3 strips, $1^1/4" \times 40"$.

From the outer-border fabric:
  Cut 4 strips, $5" \times 40"$.
From the binding fabric:
  Cut 5 strips, $3" \times 40"$.
From the hanging-sleeve fabric:
  Cut 2 strips, $8^1/2" \times 40"$.

*Adjust the size of these squares as needed to fit the embroidery hoop. Trim to $5" \times 5"$ after the embroidery is complete.

Making the Blocks

1. Follow the manufacturer's instructions for the stabilizer, and use the stabilizer to prepare each $9^1/2"$ light square for embroidery. Select an embroidery collection and embroider a different motif in the center of each stabilized square. Press and trim the embroidered square to measure $5" \times 5"$. Don't worry about the grain of the fabric; cut the square to best suit the embroidery motif. Make 9.

Make 9.

Tools for Trimming!

As an aid to trimming the embroidered square, use a 5" ruler or place tape on a larger ruler to measure off a 5" square. Center the motif in the square and trim.

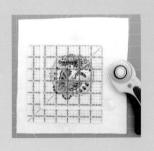

2. Sew a 1″ × 5″ accent strip to the top and bottom of each trimmed embroidered square from Step 1; press. Repeat to add a 1″ × 6″ strip to the sides; press. Make 9.

Make 9.

Press for success!
Press the embroidery right side down on a terry towel.

3. Sew 2 sets of 1³/₄″ × 20″ Attic Window strips into matching pairs; press. Make 5 matching strip sets and label them strip set A. Repeat with the remaining 2 sets of 1³/₄″ × 20″ strips, pressing the seams in the opposite direction. Label them strip set B.

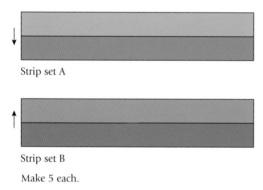

Strip set A

Strip set B

Make 5 each.

4. Cut each strip set from Step 3 in half to make twenty 3″ × 10″ segments: 10 of segment A and 10 of segment B. You will have 1 segment in each combination left over; set these aside for another project.

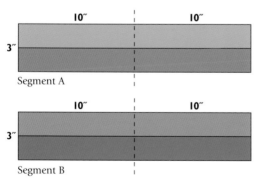

10″   10″

3″

Segment A

10″   10″

3″

Segment B

Cut 10 segments each (20 total).

5. With right sides together and top left edges aligned, pin an A segment from Step 4 to a unit from Step 2, as shown. Turn the unit over so the embroidered square is face down and sew segment A to the right edge. Stop ¹/₄″ from the bottom edge of the square with a backstitch; finger press the seam.

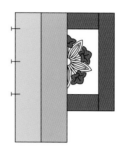

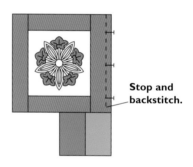

Stop and backstitch.

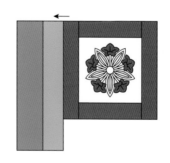

6. With right sides together and bottom and left edges aligned, pin a B segment to the bottom of the unit from Step 5 as shown. Turn the unit over so that the embroidered square is face down and sew segment B to the bottom edge, interlocking the seams. Stop with a backstitch where the stitches meet the previous line of stitching; press. Refer to Mitered Borders (page 14) to complete the corner seams.

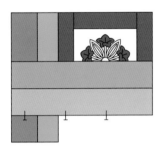

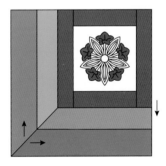

7. Repeat Steps 5 and 6 to make a total of 9 blocks.

Assembling the Quilt

1. Arrange the blocks in 3 horizontal rows of 3 blocks each, placing a $1^3/4'' \times 8^1/2''$ filler strip at the right end of rows 1 and 3 and at the left end of row 2, as shown in the assembly diagram.

2. Sew the strips and blocks into rows; press. Sew the rows together; press.

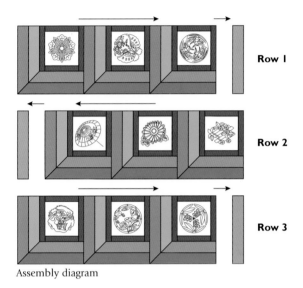

Row 1

Row 2

Row 3

Assembly diagram

3. Stitch matching $1^3/4'' \times 20''$ sashing strips, short ends together, in pairs; press. Trim each pieced strip to measure $25^3/4''$ long. Sew 1 strip to the top of the unit from Step 2. Press the seam toward the sashing strip. Sew the remaining strip to the right edge; press.

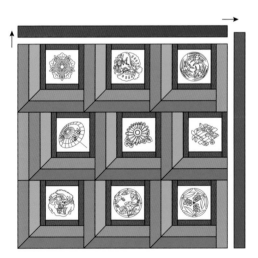

4. Refer to Squared Borders (page 14) to measure, fit, and sew a $1^1/4''$-wide inner-border strip to the top and bottom of the quilt. Press the seams toward the borders. Repeat to sew inner borders to the sides of the quilt; press.

5. Measure your quilt through the center from top to bottom and from side to side. To these measurements, add the finished width of the border ($4^1/2''$) plus $1/2''$ for the seam allowances (5″ total). Cut 2 borders to each length from the 5″-wide outer-border strips.

6. Find and mark the midpoint on each side of the quilt top. From one end of each border, measure and mark the length of the *quilt top* as determined in Step 5. Find and mark the midpoint between the end of the border and the point you've just marked, as shown.

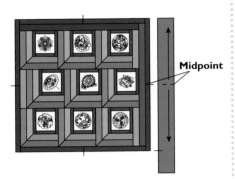

7. Place a marked border right sides together with the right edge of the quilt top. Align the top edges of the border and the quilt top and match the midpoints. Match the bottom right corner of the quilt top with the endpoint you marked on the border in Step 6; pin. The border will extend beyond the bottom edge of the quilt.

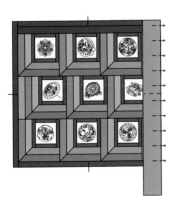

8. Sew the border to the quilt, stopping approximately 3″ from the marked corner of the quilt top; press.

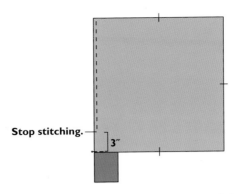

9. Place the top border and the top edge of the quilt top right sides together. Match the midpoints and the ends. Pin and sew, this time sewing the entire seam. Repeat this step to add the left and bottom borders. Complete the first seam; press.

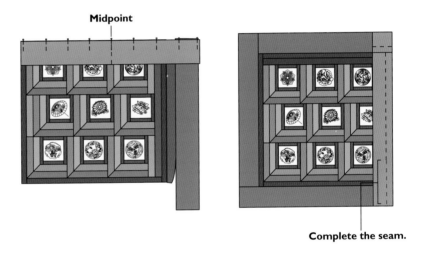

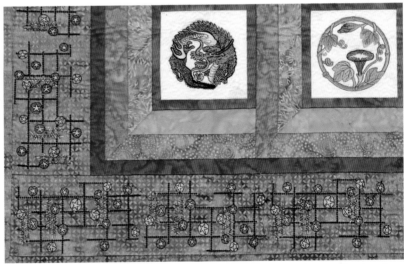

I used the fabric as inspiration for embroidered embellishment in the outer border of *Window of Opportunity*. For a full view of this quilt, see page 33.

Finishing the Quilt

Refer to Finishing Your Quilt (page 18).

1. Prepare the backing as described on page 16.

2. Layer the quilt top, batting, and backing; baste.

3. Hand or machine quilt as desired.

4. Use the 3″-wide strips to bind the edges of the quilt.

5. Add a hanging sleeve and label if desired.

Quilting and embellishing suggestions

My Favorite Quilt Blocks, 35³⁄₄″ × 35³⁄₄″, made by Susie Kincy, machine quilted by Barbara Dau, 2006.

Creative Option

Think outside the block! Repeat your favorite embroidery motifs in the outer border, either in the border strips themselves, as I did, or in embroidered cornerstones. For the latter option, you will need ²⁄₃ yard of fabric for the outer border and an additional ¹⁄₃ yard of fabric for the embroidered cornerstones.

1. Cut four 9¹⁄₂″ squares from the cornerstone fabric. Stabilize, embroider, press, and trim the blocks as described in Making the Blocks, Step 1 (page 34).

2. Cut four 5″ × 40″ strips from the crosswise grain of the outer-border fabric. Refer to Borders With Cornerstones (page 14). Measure the quilt through the center from side to side and from top to bottom. Cut 2 borders to each length from the 5″-wide outer-border strips. Fit and sew a 5″-wide border to the top and bottom of the quilt. Press the seams toward the outer borders.

3. Sew an embroidered and trimmed cornerstone from Step 1 to each end of each remaining 5″-wide strip; press. Sew the border units to the sides of the quilt; press.

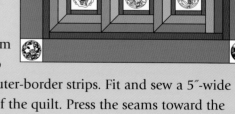

Dreams on the Mesa, $35\frac{3}{4}'' \times 35\frac{3}{4}''$, made by John and Louise James, machine quilted by Barbara Dau, 2006.

Itsy Bitsy's Treats, $35\frac{3}{4}'' \times 35\frac{3}{4}''$, made by John and Louise James, machine quilted by Barbara Dau, 2006.

Full Bloom, 35¾″ × 35¾″, designed and made by M'Liss Rae Hawley, machine quilted by Barbara Dau, 2006. Photos by Michael A. Hawley.

Scan or Load the Image

The first step is to scan or load the desired background image into 3D Sketch. If you're using a digital photograph, you can load the image directly from your picture folder on your computer. If you are working with a traditional photograph or other printed image, place it in your scanner and scan directly by clicking the scan icon.

Sketch It

Here is where the fun begins! Simply begin sketching stitches on top of the image to highlight the areas you wish to personalize, enhance, or emphasize with creative stitching. There are a variety of stitches you can use. The Free Motion stitch works just like free-motion embroidery: the faster you move the pen, the less dense the stitches become. For *Full Bloom*, I used the Free Motion stitch in the center of each flower to highlight that area. I used different types of stitches to fill in other areas of the flowers, branches, and leaves.

Print It

Once you are satisfied with your sketching, use an inkjet printer to print the background image onto printable fabric (see Resources on page 78). When you print the image, you can choose

between two options depending upon the look you prefer: print either at full-strength color or with the color a little bit faded. I printed the flower at full strength because I wanted to show the beautiful colors in the photo as well as the stitches made in the program.

Stitch It

Now simply stitch out the 3D Sketch design and you have created your own personalized design of—and on—your favorite photo. And because you now have both the image *and* the stitch file, you can repeat the embroidery again and again without having to re-create the design.

Framed in Starlight

Finished quilt: $42\frac{1}{2}'' \times 42\frac{1}{2}''$
Finished block: $7'' \times 7''$

Under Capricorn Starlight, designed and made by M'Liss Rae Hawley, machine quilted by Barbara Dau, 2006.

On clear nights, while working late in my studio, I often go out on my deck to enjoy the Milky Way, the moon, the planets, and—when I am especially lucky—shooting stars. I created the Framed in Starlight pattern as the perfect combination of earth-bound and heavenly images: sixteen Log Cabin blocks surrounded by twenty Shooting Star blocks.

This is a fun quilt! I used the color wheel and batik fabrics to create the illusion of starlight and movement.

Materials

Fat quarters require $17^1/2˝ \times 20˝$ of usable fabric. All other yardages are based on 40˝-wide fabric.

- Fat quarters of 18 assorted fabrics: 3 (1 light, 1 medium, and 1 dark) *each* of yellow, orange, red, purple, blue, and green fabric for blocks
- Additional fat quarter of the dark yellow fabric for Log Cabin center squares
- $5/8$ yard of fabric for binding
- $1/2$ yard of fabric for hanging sleeve
- 3 yards of fabric for backing
- $50˝ \times 50˝$ piece of batting

Cutting

Before cutting, sort the 18 fat quarters for the blocks by color. Within each color, sort the fabrics into 3 stacks and label them 1 (light), 2 (medium), and 3 (dark). Cut along the 20˝ length of the fat quarters. For the remaining fabrics, cut strips on the crosswise grain (from selvage to selvage).

From the orange 1 fat quarter:
　Cut 2 strips, $1^1/2˝ \times 20˝$.
From the yellow 1 fat quarter:
　Cut 2 strips, $1^1/2˝ \times 20˝$.
　Cut 12 rectangles, $2˝ \times 4˝$.
　Cut 3 squares, $2˝ \times 2˝$.

From the red 1 fat quarter:
　Cut 2 strips, $1^1/2˝ \times 20˝$.
　Cut 12 rectangles, $2˝ \times 4˝$.
　Cut 3 squares, $2˝ \times 2˝$.
From the purple 1 fat quarter:
　Cut 2 strips, $1^1/2˝ \times 20˝$.
　Cut 12 rectangles, $2˝ \times 3^1/4˝$.
　Cut 12 squares, $3^1/4˝ \times 3^1/4˝$.
From the blue 1 fat quarter:
　Cut 2 strips, $1^1/2˝ \times 20˝$.
　Cut 8 rectangles, $2˝ \times 4˝$.
　Cut 2 squares, $2˝ \times 2˝$.
From the green 1 fat quarter:
　Cut 1 strip, $1^1/2˝ \times 20˝$.
　Cut 8 rectangles, $2˝ \times 4˝$.
　Cut 2 squares, $2˝ \times 2˝$.
From the orange 2 fat quarter:
　Cut 3 strips, $1^1/2˝ \times 20˝$.
　Cut 8 rectangles, $2˝ \times 4˝$.
　Cut 2 squares, $2˝ \times 2˝$.
From the yellow 2 fat quarter:
　Cut 2 strips, $1^1/2˝ \times 20˝$.
　Cut 8 rectangles, $2˝ \times 4˝$.
　Cut 2 squares, $2˝ \times 2˝$.
From the blue 2 fat quarter:
　Cut 3 strips, $1^1/2˝ \times 20˝$.
　Cut 8 rectangles, $2˝ \times 3^1/4˝$.
　Cut 8 squares, $3^1/4˝ \times 3^1/4˝$.
From the red 2 fat quarter:
　Cut 4 strips, $1^1/2˝ \times 20˝$.
　Cut 12 rectangles, $2˝ \times 3^1/4˝$.
　Cut 12 squares, $3^1/4˝ \times 3^1/4˝$.

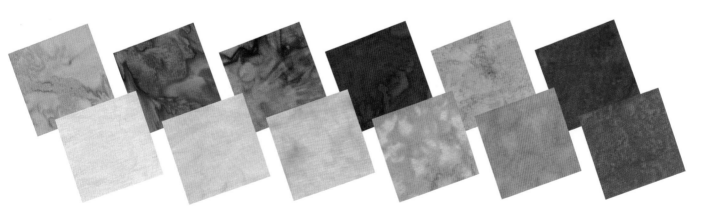

From the purple 2 fat quarter:
Cut 4 strips, $1^{1}/_{2}$″ × 20″.
Cut 12 rectangles, 2″ × 4″.
Cut 3 squares, 2″ × 2″.

From the green 2 fat quarter:
Cut 2 strips, $1^{1}/_{2}$″ × 20″.
Cut 12 rectangles, 2″ × $3^{1}/_{4}$″.
Cut 12 squares, $3^{1}/_{4}$″ × $3^{1}/_{4}$″.

From the orange 3 fat quarter:
Cut 4 strips, $1^{1}/_{2}$″ × 20″.
Cut 8 rectangles, 2″ × $3^{1}/_{4}$″.
Cut 8 squares, $3^{1}/_{4}$″ × $3^{1}/_{4}$″.

From the yellow 3 fat quarter:
Cut 3 strips, $1^{1}/_{2}$″ × 20″.
Cut 12 rectangles, 2″ × $3^{1}/_{4}$″.
Cut 12 squares, $3^{1}/_{4}$″ × $3^{1}/_{4}$″.

From the blue 3 fat quarter:
Cut 4 strips, $1^{1}/_{2}$″ × 20″.

From the red 3 fat quarter:
Cut 5 strips, $1^{1}/_{2}$″ × 20″.
Cut 8 rectangles, 2″ × $3^{1}/_{4}$″.
Cut 8 squares, $3^{1}/_{4}$″ × $3^{1}/_{4}$″.

From the purple 3 fat quarter:
Cut 5 strips, $1^{1}/_{2}$″ × 20″.
Cut 8 rectangles, 2″ × $3^{1}/_{4}$″.
Cut 8 squares, $3^{1}/_{4}$″ × $3^{1}/_{4}$″.

From the green 3 fat quarter:
Cut 3 strips, $1^{1}/_{2}$″ × 20″.
Cut 12 rectangles, 2″ × 4″.
Cut 3 squares, 2″ × 2″.

From the additional dark yellow center-square fat quarter:
Cut 2 strips, $1^{1}/_{2}$″ × 20″;
crosscut into 16 squares,
$1^{1}/_{2}$″ × $1^{1}/_{2}$″.

From the binding fabric:
Cut 5 strips, 3″ × 40″.

From the hanging-sleeve fabric:
Cut 2 strips, $8^{1}/_{2}$″ × 40″.

Creative Option

You can give this quilt a totally different look by choosing soft pastels, such as the 1930s-inspired palette Annette Barca selected for her quilt *Remembering the Past* (page 48).

Making the Log Cabin Blocks

This quilt includes sixteen 7″ Log Cabin blocks. Each block begins with a $1^{1}/_{2}$″ dark yellow center square that is surrounded by 3 rounds of $1^{1}/_{2}$″-wide strips. The strips grade in value from the lightest (1) near the center to the darkest (3) along the outside edges.

The blocks appear in 7 color combinations: 2 of block A (orange and yellow), 3 of block B (red and orange), 4 of block C (purple and red), 3 of block D (blue and purple), 2 of block E (green and blue), and 1 each of block F (yellow) and block G (green). All the blocks are constructed the same way; only the strip colors change.

Before beginning, sort the $1^{1}/_{2}$″-wide strips by color. Within each color, sort the fabrics into three stacks and label them 1 (light), 2 (medium), and 3 (dark).

Keep an iron nearby so you can press all seam allowances as you go. Press away from the center square, toward the outer edges of the block.

1. With right sides together and raw edges aligned, sew a $1^{1}/_{2}$″-wide orange 1 strip to the right edge of a $1^{1}/_{2}$″ yellow 3 center square, as shown; press. Trim the strip even with the square. Make 2.

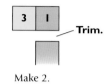

Make 2.

2. Repeat Step 1 to sew a $1^{1}/_{2}$″-wide orange 1 strip to the bottom edge of each unit; press and trim.

3. Repeat Step 1 to sew $1^{1}/_{2}$″-wide yellow 1 strips to the left and top edges of each unit; press and trim.

4. Repeat Steps 1–3 to sew 1½″-wide orange 2 and yellow 2 strips to each unit to create a second round, and 1½″-wide orange 3 and yellow 3 strips to create a third and final round. You will have 2 blocks. Label them block A.

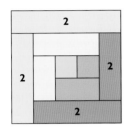

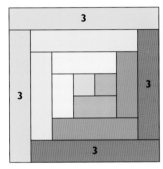

Block A
Make 2.

5. Repeat Steps 1–4 using 1½″ yellow 3 center squares, 1½″-wide red strips (1–3), and 1½″-wide orange strips (1–3). Make 3 blocks and label them block B.

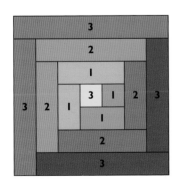

Block B
Make 3.

6. Repeat Steps 1–4 using 1½″ yellow 3 center squares, 1½″-wide purple strips (1–3), and 1½″-wide red strips (1–3). Make 4 blocks and label them block C.

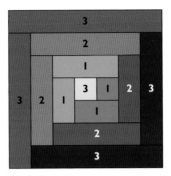

Block C
Make 4.

7. Repeat Steps 1–4 using 1½″ yellow 3 center squares, 1½″-wide blue strips (1–3), and 1½″-wide purple strips (1–3). Make 3 blocks and label them block D.

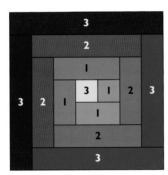

Block D
Make 3.

8. Repeat Steps 1–4 using 1½″ yellow 3 center squares, 1½″-wide green strips (1–3), and 1½″-wide blue strips (1–3). Make 2 blocks and label them block E.

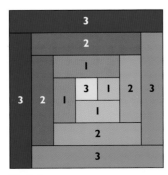

Block E
Make 2.

9. Repeat Steps 1–4 using a 1½″ yellow 3 center square and 1½″-wide yellow strips (1–3). Make 1 block and label it block F.

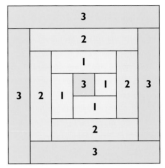

Block F
Make 1.

10. Repeat Steps 1–4 using a 1½″ yellow center square and 1½″-wide green strips (1–3). Make 1 block and label it block G.

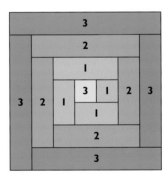

Block G
Make 1.

Detail of Log Cabin block

Making the Shooting Star Blocks

This quilt includes twenty 7″ Shooting Star blocks with "wonky" (free-form) points. The blocks appear in 8 color combinations: 3 each of block H (yellow 3 and green 3) and block I (green 2 and yellow 1), 2 each of block J (orange 3 and yellow 2) and block K (red 3 and orange 2), 3 each of block L (purple 1 and red 1) and block M (red 2 and purple 2), and 2 each of block N (purple 3 and blue 1) and block O (blue 2 and green 1). All blocks are constructed the same way; only the colors change.

1. Place matching 2″ × 4″ rectangles right sides together and cut from corner to corner on one diagonal to make the star points. You'll have 160 triangles total, 80 in each mirror image. Sort and label the triangles by color and number (1–3).

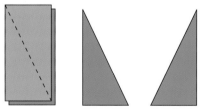

Make 160 triangles; 80 of each mirror image.

2. Place a green 3 star-point triangle right sides together with each 2″ × 3¼″ yellow 3 background rectangle on a random diagonal, as shown. Fold the green triangle back to preview the star point. When you are satisfied with the placement, finger press the green triangle to mark the ¼″ seam allowance.

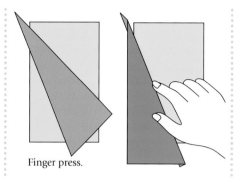

Finger press.

3. Reopen the green triangle so it is right sides together with the yellow rectangle; pin. Make 4 units for each block, angling the triangle a little differently each time.

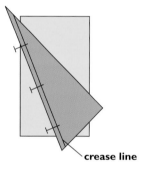

crease line

Make 4 for each block.

4. Sew directly on the crease you made in Step 2. Repeat for each unit.

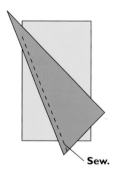

Sew.

5. Fold the green triangle back and press with an iron. Turn the unit over and trim the green rectangle even with the edges of the yellow rectangle. Repeat for each unit.

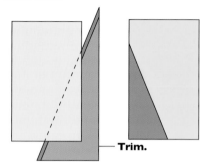

Trim.

6. Repeat Steps 2–5, using a mirror image green 3 star-point triangle for each unit. Make 4 for each block.

Make 4 for each block.

7. Arrange 4 units from Step 6, four 3¼″ yellow 3 squares, and one 2″ green 3 square in 3 rows of 3 units and squares each, as shown. Sew the units and squares into rows; press. Sew the rows together; press. Make 3 blocks and label them block H.

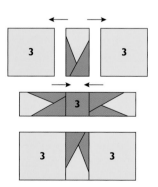

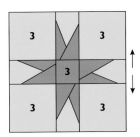

Block H
Make 3.

8. Repeat Steps 2–7 using yellow 1 star-point triangles with 2″ × 3¹/₄″ green 2 rectangles, 3¹/₄″ green 2 squares, and 2″ yellow 1 squares. Make 3 blocks and label them block I.

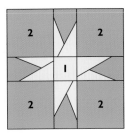

Block I
Make 3.

9. Repeat Steps 2–7 using the yellow 2 star-point triangles with 2″ × 3¹/₄″ orange 3 rectangles, 3¹/₄″ orange 3 squares, and 2″ yellow 2 squares. Make 2 blocks and label them block J.

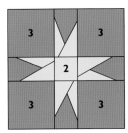

Block J
Make 2.

10. Repeat Steps 2–7 using the orange 2 star-point triangles with 2″ × 3¹/₄″ red 3 rectangles, 3¹/₄″ red 3 squares, and 2″ orange 2 squares. Make 2 blocks and label them block K.

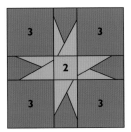

Block K
Make 2.

11. Repeat Steps 2–7 using the red 1 star-point triangles with 2″ × 3¹/₄″ purple 1 rectangles, 3¹/₄″ purple 1 squares, and 2″ red 1 squares. Make 3 blocks and label them block L.

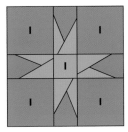

Block L
Make 3.

12. Repeat Steps 2–7 using the purple 2 star-point triangles with 2″ × 3¹/₄″ red 2 rectangles, 3¹/₄″ red 2 squares, and 2″ purple 2 squares. Make 3 blocks and label them block M.

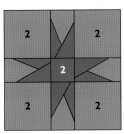

Block M
Make 3.

13. Repeat Steps 2–7 using the blue 1 star-point triangles with 2″ × 3¹/₄″ purple 3 rectangles, 3¹/₄″ purple 3 squares, and 2″ blue 1 squares. Make 2 blocks and label them block N.

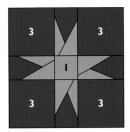

Block N
Make 2.

14. Repeat Steps 2–7 using the green 1 star-point triangles with 2″ × 3¹/₄″ blue 2 rectangles, 3¹/₄″ blue 2 squares, and 2″ green 1 squares. Make 2 blocks and label them block O.

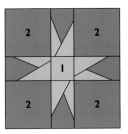

Block O
Make 2.

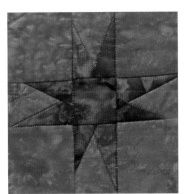

Detail of Shooting Star block

Assembling the Quilt

Arrange the Log Cabin and Shooting Star blocks in 6 horizontal rows of 6 blocks each, as shown in the assembly diagram below. Sew the blocks together into rows. Press the seams in alternating directions from row to row. Sew the rows together; press.

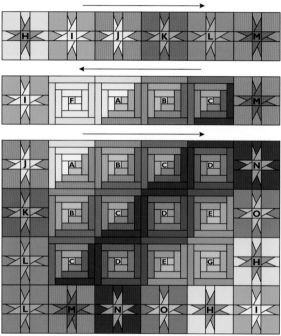

Assembly diagram

Finishing the Quilt

Refer to Finishing Your Quilt (page 18).

1. Prepare the backing as described on page 16.
2. Layer the quilt top, batting, and backing; baste.
3. Hand or machine quilt as desired.
4. Use the 3″-wide strips to bind the edges of the quilt.
5. Add a hanging sleeve and label if desired.

Quilting suggestions

Remembering the Past, 41″ × 41″, made by Annette Barca, machine quilted by Barbara Dau, 2006.

Tropical Vacation,
43″ × 43″, made by Susie
Kincy, machine quilted by
Barbara Dau, 2006.

Reminiscent,
43″ × 43″, made by
Susie Kincy, machine
quilted by Barbara Dau,
2006.

Garden Gate

Finished quilt: $37\frac{1}{4}'' \times 55\frac{1}{4}''$

A Place to Ponder, designed and made by M'Liss Rae Hawley, machine quilted by Barbara Dau, 2006.

The Garden Gate pattern is fast and easy—a great size for a wall-hanging or baby quilt. The seven fat quarters create a reflection, or mirror image. One fat quarter runs through the center, and the remaining six repeat on either side.

My husband, Michael, and I are avid gardeners, and *A Place to Ponder* is reminiscent of our garden. The optional cornerstones are a perfect showcase for embroideries that continue the theme of the quilt.

Materials

Fat quarters require $17^{1}/_{2}" \times 20"$ of usable fabric. All other yardages are based on 40"-wide fabric.

Note: *For this quilt, avoid fat quarters with a one-way (directional) print that runs parallel to the 17" edge of the fabric. If you select a fat quarter with a one-way print, be sure the direction of the print runs parallel to the 20" edge. That way, all the fence posts will run vertically when the strata (strip sets) are pieced, crosscut, and placed in the quilt.*

- $^{1}/_{2}$ yard of fabric for background and inner border
- Fat quarters of 7 fabrics in assorted values for fence rails*
- $^{2}/_{3}$ yard of fabric for outer border
- Fat quarter of fabric for border cornerstones
- $^{5}/_{8}$ yard of fabric for binding
- $^{1}/_{3}$ yard of fabric for hanging sleeve
- $3^{5}/_{8}$ yards of fabric for backing
- $45" \times 63"$ piece of batting
- * Label these fabrics 1–7.

Cutting

Cut along the 20" length of the fat quarters. For the remaining fabrics, cut strips on the crosswise grain (from selvage to selvage).

From the background and inner-border fabric:
Cut 1 strip, $2^{1}/_{2}" \times 40"$; crosscut into 2 strips, $2^{1}/_{2}" \times 20"$.
Cut 5 strips, $1^{3}/_{4}" \times 40"$.

From *each* of fat quarters 1–6:
Cut 2 strips, $5^{3}/_{4}" \times 20"$.
Cut 2 strips, $1^{3}/_{4}" \times 20"$.

From fat quarter 7:
Cut 1 strip, $5^{3}/_{4}" \times 20"$.
Cut 1 strip, $1^{3}/_{4}" \times 20"$.

From the outer-border fabric:
Cut 4 strips, $4^{1}/_{2}" \times 40"$.

From the border cornerstone fabric:*
Cut 4 squares, $4^{1}/_{2}" \times 4^{1}/_{2}"$.

From the binding fabric:
Cut 6 strips, $3" \times 40"$.

From the hanging-sleeve fabric:
Cut 1 strip, $8^{1}/_{2}" \times 40"$.

* *If you plan to embroider these squares as I have, cut them $9" \times 9"$ or large enough to fit your hoop. (You'll need $^{1}/_{3}$ yard of fabric.) Trim them to $4^{1}/_{2}" \times 4^{1}/_{2}"$ after the embroidery is complete.*

Assembling the Quilt

1. Arrange a $2^{1}/_{2}" \times 20"$ background strip, a $1^{3}/_{4}" \times 20"$ fabric 1 strip, a $5^{3}/_{4}" \times 20"$ fabric 2 strip, a $1^{3}/_{4}" \times 20"$ fabric 3 strip, a $5^{3}/_{4}" \times 20"$ fabric 4 strip, a $1^{3}/_{4}" \times 20"$ fabric 5 strip, a $5^{3}/_{4}" \times 20"$ fabric 6 strip, a $1^{3}/_{4}" \times 20"$ fabric 7 strip, a $5^{3}/_{4}" \times 20"$ fabric 6 strip, a $1^{3}/_{4}" \times 20"$ fabric 5 strip, a $5^{3}/_{4}" \times 20"$ fabric 4 strip, a $1^{3}/_{4}" \times 20"$ fabric 3 strip, a $5^{3}/_{4}" \times 20"$ fabric 2 strip, a $1^{3}/_{4}" \times 20"$ fabric 1 strip, and a $2^{1}/_{2}" \times 20"$ background strip in order, as shown. With right sides together, sew the strips together to make a strip set (or strata); press the seams toward the wide strips. Label this strata A.

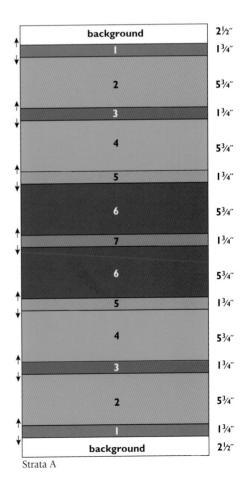

background	$2^{1}/_{2}"$
1	$1^{3}/_{4}"$
2	$5^{3}/_{4}"$
3	$1^{3}/_{4}"$
4	$5^{3}/_{4}"$
5	$1^{3}/_{4}"$
6	$5^{3}/_{4}"$
7	$1^{3}/_{4}"$
6	$5^{3}/_{4}"$
5	$1^{3}/_{4}"$
4	$5^{3}/_{4}"$
3	$1^{3}/_{4}"$
2	$5^{3}/_{4}"$
1	$1^{3}/_{4}"$
background	$2^{1}/_{2}"$

Strata A

2. Arrange a $5^3/4″ \times 20″$ fabric 1 strip, a $1^3/4″ \times 20″$ fabric 2 strip, a $5^3/4″ \times 20″$ fabric 3 strip, a $1^3/4″ \times 20″$ fabric 4 strip, a $5^3/4″ \times 20″$ fabric 5 strip, a $1^3/4″ \times 20″$ fabric 6 strip, a $5^3/4″ \times 20″$ fabric 7 strip, a $1^3/4″ \times 20″$ fabric 6 strip, a $5^3/4″ \times 20″$ fabric 5 strip, a $1^3/4″ \times 20″$ fabric 4 strip, a $5^3/4″ \times 20″$ fabric 3 strip, a $1^3/4″ \times 20″$ fabric 2 strip, and a $5^3/4″ \times 20″$ fabric 1 strip in order, as shown. With right sides together, sew the strips together to make a strip set (or strata); press the seams toward the wide strips. Label this strata B.

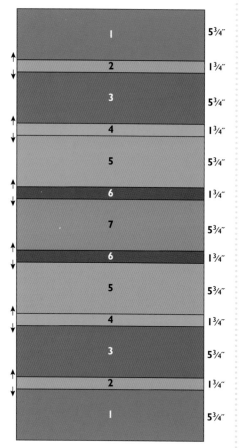

Strata B

3. Crosscut strata A into eleven $1^3/4″$-wide segments. Label these segment A.

4. Crosscut strata B into ten $1^3/4″$-wide segments. Label these segment B.

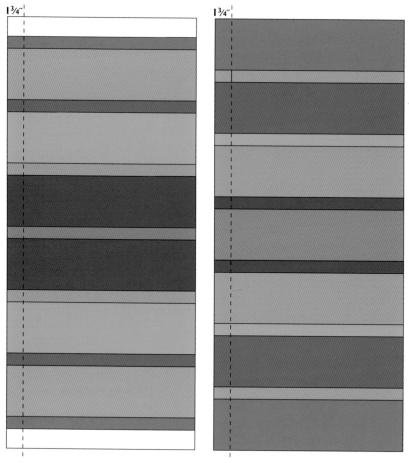

Segment A. Cut 11 segments. Segment B. Cut 10 segments.

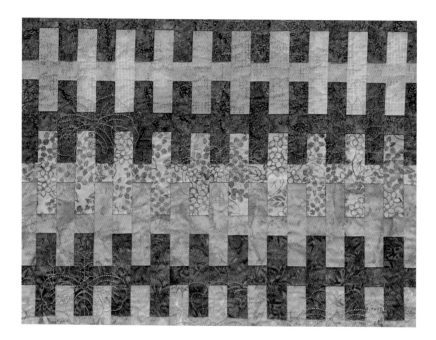

5. Beginning with an A segment from Step 3, arrange the A and B segments, alternating them as shown in the assembly diagram below. With right sides together, sew the segments together. Press the seams toward the B segments.

A B A B A B A B A B A B A B A B A B A B A

Assembly diagram

6. Refer to Squared Borders (page 14) to measure, fit, and sew a 1³/₄″-wide background inner-border strip to the top and bottom of the quilt. Press the seams toward the borders. Repeat to sew inner borders to the sides of the quilt, piecing as necessary; press.

7. If you wish, embroider a favorite motif in each 9″ border corner-stone square. (See Tips for Machine Embroidery on page 12 for guidance and Resources on page 78 for the embroideries I used in my quilt.) Press and trim the embroidered blocks to 4¹/₂″ × 4¹/₂″.

8. Refer to Borders With Cornerstones (page 14). Measure the quilt through the center from side to side and from top to bottom. Fit and sew a 4¹/₂″-wide outer-border strip to the top and bottom of the quilt, using the side-to-side measurement, and piecing as necessary. Press the seams toward the borders.

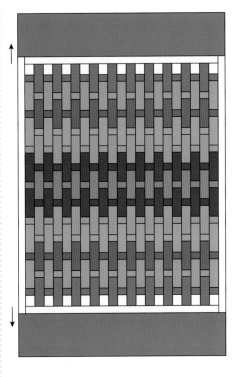

9. Cut two 4½˝-wide outer-border strips using the top-to-bottom measurement you obtained in Step 8, piecing as necessary. Sew a 4½˝ embroidered and trimmed or plain border cornerstone to each end of each strip; press. Sew the border units to the sides of the quilt; press.

Make 2.

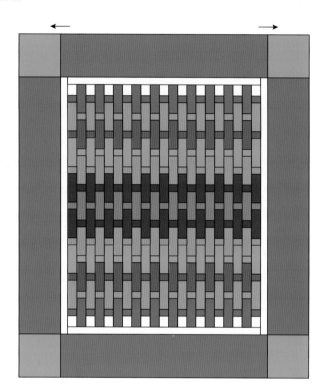

Creative Option

You'll need ⅞ yard of border fabric for this option. For an example, see *Winter Garden* (page 55), a quilt my sister Erin and I made. Cut 5 strips, 4½˝ × 40˝, on the crosswise grain. Refer to Squared Borders (page 14) to measure, fit, and sew a 4½˝-wide border strip to the top and bottom of the quilt, piecing as necessary. Press the seams toward the borders. Repeat to sew borders to the sides of the quilt; press.

Finishing the Quilt

Refer to Finishing Your Quilt (page 18).

1. Prepare the backing as described on page 16.

2. Layer the quilt top, batting, and backing; baste.

3. Hand or machine quilt as desired.

4. Use the 3˝-wide strips to bind the edges of the quilt.

5. Add a hanging sleeve and label if desired.

Quilting suggestions

Winter Garden, 36¹/₂″ × 54″,
designed by M'Liss Rae Hawley,
made by M'Liss Rae Hawley and
Erin Rae Vautier, machine quilted
by Barbara Dau, 2006.

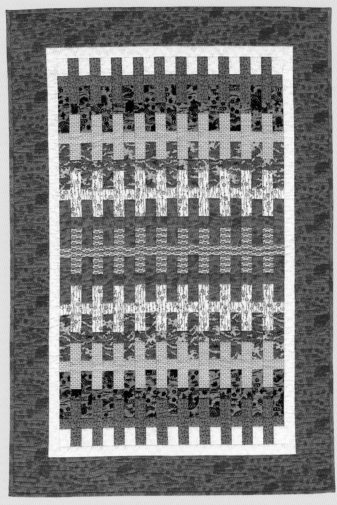

The Aroma of Exotic Spices,
36″ × 56″, made by Carla Zimmermann,
machine quilted by Arlene Anderson, 2006.

Esther's Garden, 36″ × 54″, made by Susie Kincy, machine quilted by Barbara Dau, 2006.

A Cottage in Provence, 38″ × 56″, made and machine quilted by Marie L. Miller, 2006.

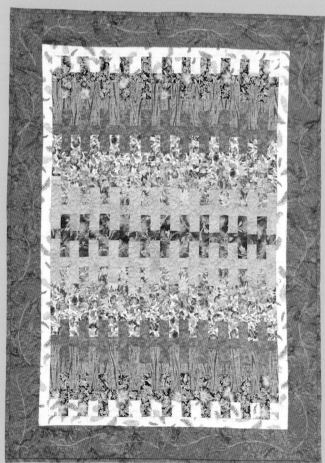

Purple Garden, 36″ × 56″, made by Anastasia Riordan, machine quilted by Barbara Dau, 2006.

Parallel Paths

Finished quilt: $50\frac{1}{2}'' \times 67\frac{1}{2}''$

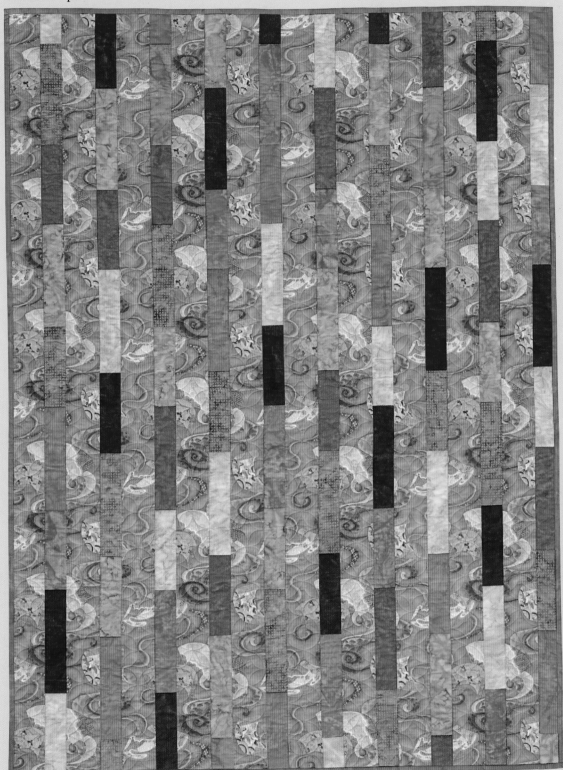

A Path Less Traveled, designed and made by M'Liss Rae Hawley, machine quilted by Barbara Dau, 2006.

Parallel Paths is the easiest pattern in the book. It is fast and fun—no blocks and no borders! You simply alternate pieced columns with $3\frac{1}{2}$"-wide strips of theme or background fabric to complete the quilt. What could be simpler?

A *Path Less Traveled* mixes batiks with selections from my Kimono Art II fabric collection in a unique combination of vivid colors. It truly captures my lifelong love of adventure.

Materials

Fat quarters require $17\frac{1}{2}$" × 20" of usable fabric. All other yardages are based on 40"-wide fabric.

- Fat quarters of 7 assorted fabrics, ranging in value from medium to dark, for pieced columns
- 2 yards of theme or background fabric for strips
- $4\frac{1}{4}$ yards of fabric for backing
- $3/4$ yard of fabric for binding
- $1/2$ yard of fabric for hanging sleeve
- 58" × 75" piece of batting

Cutting

Cut along the 20" length of the fat quarters. For the remaining fabric, cut strips on the crosswise grain (from selvage to selvage) unless instructed otherwise.

From *each* fat quarter:
Cut 7 strips, $2\frac{1}{2}$" × 20" (49 total); crosscut into:
6 rectangles, $2\frac{1}{2}$" × $9\frac{1}{2}$" (42 total; you will have 2 left over);
6 rectangles, $2\frac{1}{2}$" × $7\frac{1}{2}$" (42 total; you will have 2 left over);
2 rectangles, $2\frac{1}{2}$" × $3\frac{1}{2}$" (14 total; you will have 4 left over).

From the *lengthwise grain* of the theme or background fabric:
Cut 10 strips, $3\frac{1}{2}$" × $67\frac{1}{2}$".

From the binding fabric:
Cut 7 strips, 3" × 40".

From the hanging-sleeve fabric:
Cut 2 strips, $8\frac{1}{2}$" × 40".

Assembling the Quilt

1. With right sides together, sew 9 assorted $2\frac{1}{2}$"-wide fat-quarter rectangles together end to end in the following order: $2\frac{1}{2}$" × $7\frac{1}{2}$", $2\frac{1}{2}$" × $9\frac{1}{2}$", $2\frac{1}{2}$" × $7\frac{1}{2}$", $2\frac{1}{2}$" × $9\frac{1}{2}$", $2\frac{1}{2}$" × $7\frac{1}{2}$", $2\frac{1}{2}$" × $9\frac{1}{2}$", $2\frac{1}{2}$" × $7\frac{1}{2}$", $2\frac{1}{2}$" × $9\frac{1}{2}$", and $2\frac{1}{2}$" × $3\frac{1}{2}$"; press. Make 5 scrappy rows and label them column A.

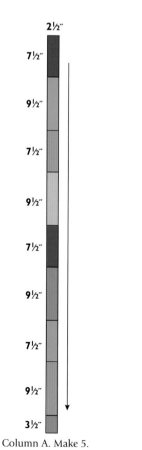

Column A. Make 5.

2. Repeat Step 1 to sew 9 assorted $2\frac{1}{2}$"-wide fat-quarter rectangles together end to end in the following order: $2\frac{1}{2}$" × $3\frac{1}{2}$", $2\frac{1}{2}$" × $9\frac{1}{2}$", $2\frac{1}{2}$" × $7\frac{1}{2}$", $2\frac{1}{2}$" × $9\frac{1}{2}$", $2\frac{1}{2}$" × $7\frac{1}{2}$", $2\frac{1}{2}$" × $9\frac{1}{2}$", $2\frac{1}{2}$" × $7\frac{1}{2}$", $2\frac{1}{2}$" × $9\frac{1}{2}$", and $2\frac{1}{2}$" × $7\frac{1}{2}$"; press. Make 5 scrappy rows and label them column B.

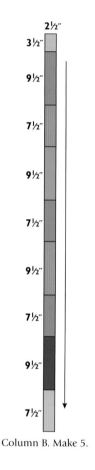

Column B. Make 5.

3. Arrange the $3\frac{1}{2}$"-wide theme or background strips and the A and B columns, alternating them as shown in the assembly diagram. Sew the strips and columns together; press.

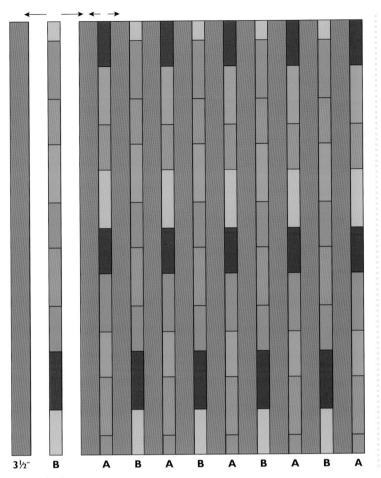

3½″ B   A   B   A   B   A   B   A   B   A

Assembly diagram

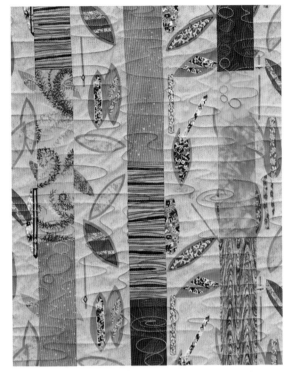

Finishing the Quilt

Refer to Finishing Your Quilt (page 18).

1. Prepare the backing as described on page 16.
2. Layer the quilt top, batting, and backing; baste.
3. Hand or machine quilt as desired.
4. Use the 3″-wide strips to bind the edges of the quilt.
5. Add a hanging sleeve and label if desired.

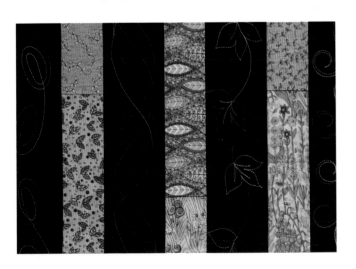

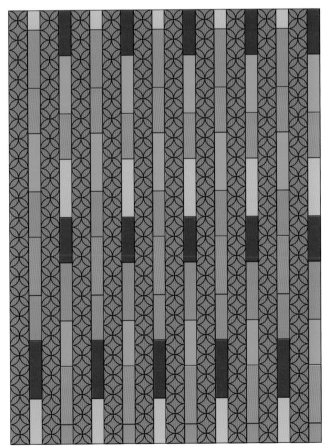

Quilting suggestions

Anacortes Adagio,
50˝ × 67˝, made by John
James, machine quilted by
Arlene Anderson, 2006.

Autumn Paths, 50˝ × 67˝, made by
Anastasia Riordan, machine quilted by
Barbara Dau, 2006.

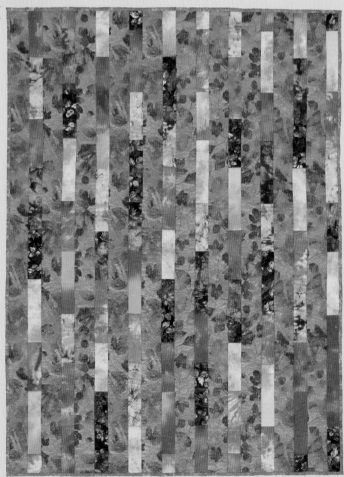

Oregon Trail,
50″ × 67″, made by
Vicki DeGraaf, machine
quilted by Stacie
Johnson and Debbie
Webster, 2006.

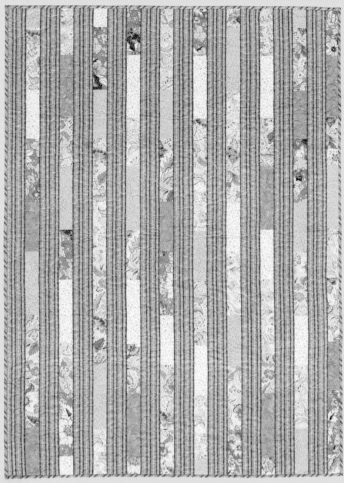

Bright Stripes,
50″ × 67″, made by Annette
Barca, machine quilted by
Barbara Dau, 2006.

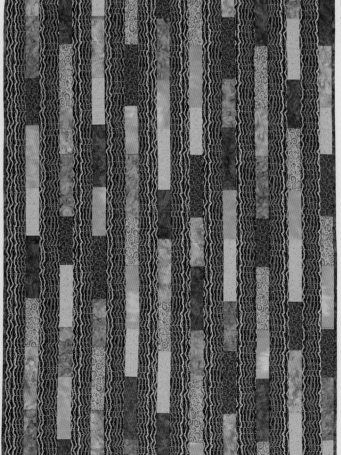

Where Have All the
Surfers Gone? 50″ × 67″,
made by Carla Zimmermann,
machine quilted by
Arlene Anderson, 2006.

Trailing Flowers,
50″ × 67″, made by Susie
Kincy, machine quilted by
Barbara Dau, 2006.

Pony Express Star

Finished quilt: $65^{1}/_{2}'' \times 78^{1}/_{2}''$
Finished block: $12'' \times 12''$

Deputy Sheriff, designed and made by M'Liss Rae Hawley, machine quilted by Barbara Dau, 2005.

I love this block! The Pony Express Star uses six fat quarters to create a 36-patch square in the center of each star. The fabrics are staggered in a Streak of Lightning format. Sashing with cornerstones separates the blocks.

A theme is a great starting point for this project. My quilt *Deputy Sheriff* is a reminder of my visit to a guild in San Antonio, Texas. My daughter, Adrienne, and I also visited the Alamo, and the fabrics I used reflect the history of the era. For a while, I considered calling my quilt *Texas Ranger*, but my husband, the sheriff of our county, insisted on its current title.

Materials

Fat quarters require $17^1/2'' \times 20''$ of usable fabric. All other yardages are based on 40″-wide fabric. See Creative Options (page 68) for additional border options.

- Fat quarters of 6 assorted fabrics for block centers
- 1 yard of fabric for star points
- 2 yards of fabric for block backgrounds
- $7/8$ yard of fabric for sashing
- $1/4$ yard of fabric for lattice cornerstones
- 1 yard each of 2 fabrics for outer border
- Fat quarter of fabric for border cornerstones
- $7/8$ yard of fabric for binding
- $1/2$ yard of fabric for hanging sleeve
- $4^7/8$ yards of fabric for backing
- $73'' \times 86''$ piece of batting

Cutting

Cut along the $17^1/2''$ length of the fat quarters. For the remaining fabrics, cut strips on the crosswise grain (from selvage to selvage).

From *each* fat quarter:
Cut 12 strips, $1^1/2'' \times 17^1/2''$.

From the star-point fabric:
Cut 8 strips, $3^7/8'' \times 40''$; crosscut into 80 squares, $3^7/8'' \times 3^7/8''$. Cut each square in half once diagonally to make 160 half-square triangles.

From the background fabric:
Cut 4 strips, $7^1/4'' \times 40''$; crosscut into 20 squares, $7^1/4'' \times 7^1/4''$. Cut each square in half twice diagonally to make 80 quarter-square triangles. Cut 8 strips, $3^1/2'' \times 40''$; crosscut into 80 squares, $3^1/2'' \times 3^1/2''$.

From the sashing fabric:
Cut 17 strips, $1^1/2'' \times 40''$; crosscut into 49 strips, $1^1/2'' \times 12^1/2''$.

From the lattice-cornerstone fabric:
Cut 2 strips, $1^1/2'' \times 40''$; crosscut into 30 squares, $1^1/2'' \times 1^1/2''$.

From *each* of border fabrics 1 and 2:
Cut 4 strips, $6^1/2'' \times 40''$ (8 total).

From the border-cornerstone fabric:
Cut 2 squares, $6^1/2'' \times 6^1/2''$.

From the binding fabric:
Cut 8 strips, $3'' \times 40''$.

From the hanging-sleeve fabric:
Cut 2 strips, $8^1/2'' \times 40''$.

Creative Option To give your quilt a scrappier look, use three different fabrics for the star points.

Making the Blocks

1. Sort the $1^1/2''$-wide fat-quarter strips by fabric and label the stacks from 1 to 6. With right sides together, sew the strips together in the following order to make 2 strip sets (or strata) of each (12 total):

1 – 2 – 3 – 4 – 5 – 6; press the seams toward fat quarter 1.

6 – 1 – 2 – 3 – 4 – 5; press the seams toward fat quarter 5.

5 – 6 – 1 – 2 – 3 – 4; press the seams toward fat quarter 5.

4 – 5 – 6 – 1 – 2 – 3; press the seams toward fat quarter 3.

3 – 4 – 5 – 6 – 1 – 2; press the seams toward fat quarter 3.

2 – 3 – 4 – 5 – 6 – 1; press the seams toward fat quarter 1.

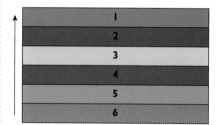

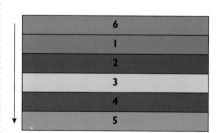

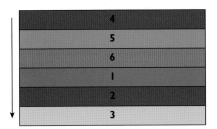

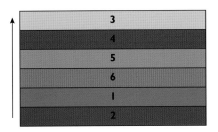

Make 2 strips sets each (12 total).

2. Crosscut each strip set from Step 1 into ten $1\frac{1}{2}$"-wide segments (20 of each strata combination, 120 total).

1½″

Cut 20 segments each (120 total).

3. Arrange and sew 1 of each segment from Step 2 together, as shown. Make 20.

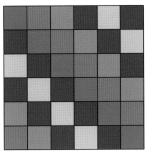

Make 20.

4. With right sides together, sew a $3\frac{7}{8}$" half-square star-point triangle to one short side of each $7\frac{1}{4}$" background quarter-square triangle, as shown; press. Repeat to sew a matching half-square triangle to the other short side of the quarter-square triangle; press. Make 80 in matching sets of 4.

Make 80.

5. Sew a matching unit from Step 4 to opposite sides of each unit from Step 3; press.

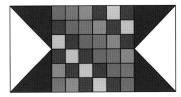

Make 20.

6. Sew each remaining unit from Step 4 between two $3\frac{1}{2}$" background squares; press.

Make 40.

7. Sew a matching unit to the remaining sides of each unit from Step 5; press. Make 20.

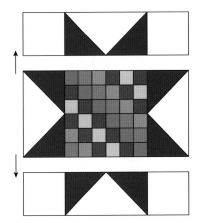

Make 20.

Assembling the Quilt

1. Sew five $1\frac{1}{2}'' \times 12\frac{1}{2}''$ lattice strips and 4 blocks together, alternating the blocks and strips to make a block row, as shown; press. Make 5 rows.

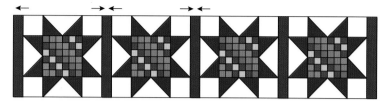

Make 5.

2. Sew four $1\frac{1}{2}'' \times 12\frac{1}{2}''$ lattice strips and five $1\frac{1}{2}''$ lattice fabric cornerstones together, alternating them to make a lattice row, as shown; press. Make 6 rows.

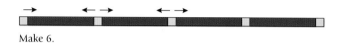

Make 6.

3. Lay out the block rows and lattice rows, alternating them as shown in the assembly diagram below. Sew the rows together; press.

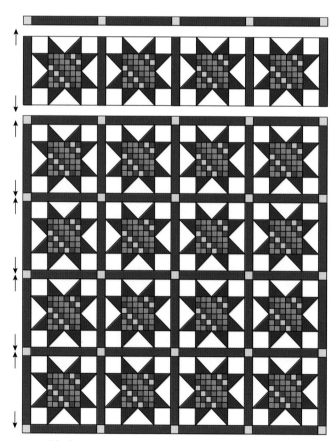

Assembly diagram

4. Refer to Borders With Cornerstones (page 14). Measure the quilt through the center from side to side and from top to bottom. Measure, fit, and sew a $6\frac{1}{2}''$-wide border fabric 1 strip to the top of the quilt, using the side-to-side measurement and piecing as necessary. Press the seams toward the border.

5. Cut a 6½″-wide fabric 1 border strip, using the top-to-bottom measurement you obtained in Step 4 and piecing as necessary. Sew a 6½″ border cornerstone to the strip, as shown; press. Sew the border unit to the right edge of the quilt; press.

6. Measure the quilt from side to side, including the border just added. Measure, fit, and sew a 6½″-wide fabric 2 border strip to the bottom of the quilt; press.

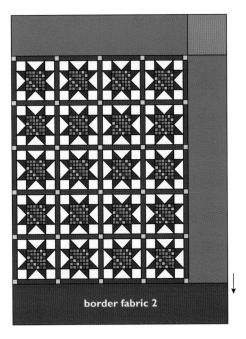

7. Measure the quilt from top to bottom, including the borders already added. Use this measurement to cut a 6¹⁄₂″-wide fabric 2 border strip, piecing as necessary. Sew a 6¹⁄₂″ border cornerstone to the strip. Sew the border unit to the left edge of the quilt; press.

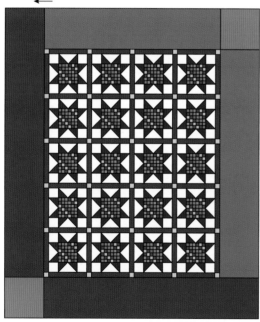

Finishing the Quilt

Refer to Finishing Your Quilt (page 18).

1. Prepare the backing as described on page 16.
2. Layer the quilt top, batting, and backing; baste.
3. Hand or machine quilt as desired.
4. Use the 3″-wide strips to bind the edges of the quilt.
5. Add a hanging sleeve and label if desired.

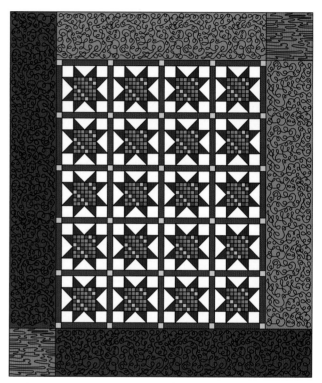

Quilting suggestions

Here are some additional options for the borders for this quilt. I'll bet you can come up with lots of other possibilities!

- Squared borders—You'll need 1¹/₂ yards of a single border fabric for this option. For an example, see Susie Kincy's quilt *Prairie Wagon Star* (below). Cut 7 strips, 6¹/₂″ × 40″, on the crosswise grain. Refer to Squared Borders (page 14) to measure, fit, and sew a 6¹/₂″-wide border strip to the top and bottom of the quilt, piecing as necessary. Press the seams toward the borders. Repeat to sew borders to the sides of the quilt; press.

- Borders With Cornerstones—You'll need 1¹/₃ yards of a single border fabric and a fat quarter of cornerstone fabric for this option. For an example, see Carla Zimmermann's quilt *Oriental Stars Shining Above Red Mountain* (page 70). Cut 6 strips, 6¹/₂″ × 40″, on the crosswise grain. Refer to Borders With Cornerstones (page 14). Measure the quilt through the center from side to side and from top to bottom. Fit and sew a 6¹/₂″-wide border strip to the top and bottom of the quilt, using the side-to-side measurement and piecing as necessary. Press the seams toward the borders. Cut 6¹/₂″-wide border strips using the top-to-bottom measurement you obtained above and piecing as necessary. Cut four 6¹/₂″ × 6¹/₂″ border cornerstones and sew one to each end of each strip; press. Sew the border units to the sides of the quilt; press.

- Embroidered Cornerstones—For added texture and visual interest, embroider the cornerstones before adding them to the quilt. See Tips for Machine Embroidery (page 12) for additional information and John James's quilt *Pony Espresso* (page 71) for an example of this border treatment.

Prairie Wagon Star, 68″ × 81″, made by Susie Kincy, machine quilted by Barbara Dau, 2006.

Star Light Star Bright, 68″ × 81″, made by Anastasia Riordan, machine quilted by Barbara Dau, 2006.

Oriental Stars Shining Above Red Mountain, 65″ × 78″, made by Carla Zimmermann, machine quilted by Barbara Dau, 2006.

Pony Espresso, 64$^1/_2$″ × 77″, made by John James, embroidered by Susie Kincy, machine quilted by Kim McKinnon, 2006.

Oregon-Idaho Express, 65″ × 79″, made by Annette Barca, machine quilted by Barbara Dau, 2006.

Showcase

Finished quilt: $43\frac{1}{2}'' \times 59\frac{1}{2}''$
Finished block: $8'' \times 8''$

Harlequin Carnival, designed and made by M'Liss Rae Hawley, machine quilted by Barbara Dau, 2002.

Showcase makes a great project for displaying theme fabrics. The center square is showcased with triangles cut from an accent fabric, and then eight fat quarters are cut into quarter-square triangles that are stitched into pairs to surround the center unit. As the blocks are joined, a secondary pattern begins to emerge.

Harlequin Carnival is a reminder of times I spent in New Orleans as an exchange student in high school and later on business trips. The palette expresses the energy and excitement of Mardi Gras and the many other festivals and activities the city hosts.

Materials

Fat quarters require $17^1/_2" \times 20"$ of usable fabric. All other yardages are based on 40"-wide fabric.

- $^1/_2$ yard of fabric for block centers
- $^2/_3$ yard of accent fabric for blocks
- Fat quarters of 8 assorted fabrics for blocks
- $^1/_4$ yard of fabric for inner border
- $1^1/_2$ yards of fabric for outer border and binding
- $^1/_2$ yard of fabric for hanging sleeve
- 4 yards of fabric for backing
- $51" \times 67"$ piece of batting

Cutting

Cut along the 20" length of the fat quarters. For the remaining fabrics, cut strips on the crosswise grain (from selvage to selvage).

From the center-square fabric:
Cut 3 strips, $4^1/_2" \times 40"$; crosscut into 24 squares, $4^1/_2" \times 4^1/_2"$.

From the accent fabric:
Cut 5 strips, $3^3/_4" \times 40"$; crosscut into 48 squares, $3^3/_4" \times 3^3/_4"$. Cut each square in half once diagonally to make 96 half-square triangles.

From *each* fat quarter:
Cut 2 strips, $5^1/_4" \times 20"$; crosscut into 6 squares, $5^1/_4" \times 5^1/_4"$. Cut each square in half twice diagonally to make 24 quarter-square triangles (192 total).

From the inner-border fabric:
Cut 5 strips, $1" \times 40"$.

From the outer-border and binding fabric:
Cut 5 strips, $5^1/_2" \times 40"$.
Cut 6 strips, $3" \times 40"$.

From the hanging-sleeve fabric:
Cut 2 strips, $8^1/_2" \times 40"$.

Making the Blocks

1. Stitch $3^3/_4"$ accent-fabric triangles to opposite sides of each $4^1/_2"$ center square; press. Add $3^3/_4"$ accent-fabric triangles to the remaining sides; press. Trim the unit to measure $6^1/_4"$, making sure to maintain the $^1/_4"$ seam allowance on all sides. Make 24.

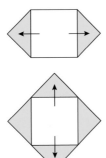

Make 24.

2. Sew 2 assorted $5^1/_4"$ quarter-square triangles together, as shown; press. Make 24 identical pairs. Repeat using the remaining $5^1/_4"$ quarter-square triangles to make a total of 96 units in matching sets of 24. Press the seams in the same direction for each pair.

Make 24 in each color combination (96 total).

3. Sew a different unit from Step 2 to opposite sides of each unit from Step 1; press. Add 1 of each remaining unit from Step 2 to the remaining sides; press. Make 24, placing the units from Step 2 in the same position in every block.

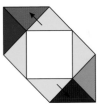

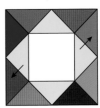

Make 24.

Assembling the Quilt

1. Arrange the blocks in 6 horizontal rows of 4 blocks each, as shown in the assembly diagram below. Sew the blocks together into rows. Press the seams in alternating directions from row to row. Sew the rows together; press.

Assembly diagram

2. Refer to Squared Borders (page 14) to measure, fit, and sew a 1″-wide inner-border strip to the top and bottom of the quilt, piecing as necessary. Press the seams toward the borders. Repeat to sew inner borders to the sides of the quilt; press the seams toward the borders.

3. Repeat Step 2 to measure, trim, and sew the 5¹/₂″-wide outer borders to the quilt, piecing as necessary. Press the seams toward the outer borders.

Finishing the Quilt

Refer to Finishing Your Quilt (page 18).

1. Prepare the backing as described on page 16.
2. Layer the quilt top, batting, and backing; baste.
3. Hand or machine quilt as desired.
4. Use the 3″-wide strips to bind the edges of the quilt.
5. Add a hanging sleeve and label if desired.

Creative Option

For a whimsical, colorful binding, cut the remaining fat quarter scraps into 3″ strips to total approximately 220″ and piece them together with diagonal seams.

Quilting suggestions

1. Refer to Borders With Cornerstones (page 14). Measure the quilt through the center from side to side and from top to bottom. Fit and sew a 5½″-wide outer-border strip to the top and bottom of the quilt, using the side-to-side measurement and piecing as necessary. Press the seams toward the borders.

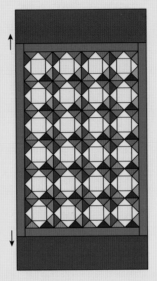

2. Cut two 5½″-wide outer-border strips, using the top-to-bottom measurement you obtained in Step 1 and piecing as necessary. Sew a 5½″ square to each end of each strip; press. Sew the border units to the sides of the quilt; press.

Make 2.

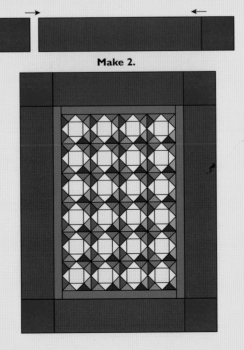

Flight of the Dragon Flies,
42″ × 56″, made by Leslie
Rommann, machine quilted by
Peggy Wilbur, 2006.

Chicago Jazz Scene,
44″ × 60″, made by
Carla Zimmermann,
machine quilted by
Cleo Andreason, 2006.

A Pilgrim's Feast,
44″ × 60″, made by Susie
Kincy, machine quilted by
Barbara Dau, 2006.

Wine in a Box,
42″ × 57″, made by John
and Louise James,
machine quilted by
Shelley Whitthal, 2006.

Sources and Information for Products Referenced

For fat quarters and other quilting supplies:

THE COTTON PATCH
3405 Hall Lane, Dept. CTB
Lafayette, CA 94549
(800) 835–4418
(925) 283–7883
quiltusa@yahoo.com
www.quiltusa.com

For fat-quarter packets via mail order and the Internet:

CONNECTING THREADS
13118 NE 4th Street
Vancouver, WA 98684
(800) 574–6454
www.connectingthreads.com

KEEPSAKE QUILTING
P.O. Box 1618
Center Harbor, NH 03226
(800) 865–9458
customerservice@keepsakequilting.com
www.keepsakequilting.com

BIG HORN QUILTS
P.O. Box 566
Greybull, WY 82426
(877) 586–9150
www.bighornquilts.com
Note: Fabric manufacturers discontinue fabrics regularly. Exact fabrics shown may no longer be available.

For information about thread:

ROBISON-ANTON TEXTILE COMPANY
P.O. Box 159
Fairview, NJ 07022
(201) 941-0500
www.robison-anton.com

For information about Sulky products:

SULKY OF AMERICA
P.O. Box 494129
Port Charlotte, FL 33949–4129
(800) 874–4115
info@sulky.com
www.sulky.com

For information about 3D Sketch embroidery software and for your nearest Husqvarna Viking dealer:

HUSQVARNA VIKING
www.husqvarnaviking.com

For information about Printed Treasures printable fabric:

MILLIKEN & COMPANY
P.O. Box 1926
Spartanburg, SC 29304
info@printedtreasures.com
www.milliken.com

For information about The Electric Quilt:

THE ELECTRIC QUILT COMPANY
419 Gould Street, Suite 2
Bowling Green, OH 43402
www.electricquilt.com

Embroidery Collections

These and other embroidery collections are available at your participating local Husqvarna Viking and Pfaff sewing machine dealers.

Kimono Art, by M'Liss Rae Hawley, Disk Part #756 259800, Inspira collection, multiformat CD-ROM

Kimono Art II, by M'Liss Rae Hawley, Disk Part #620 037296, Inspira collection, multiformat CD-ROM

My Favorite Quilt Designs, by M'Liss Rae Hawley, Disk Part #756 253300, Inspira collection, multiformat CD-ROM

Quilting With M'Liss, by M'Liss Rae Hawley, Husqvarna Viking Embroidery 175

Spring View, by M'Liss Rae Hawley, Disk Part #756 255100, Inspira collection, multiformat CD-ROM

Textures & Techniques With M'Liss, by M'Liss Rae Hawley, Husqvarna Viking Embroidery 181

Around the Yard, EZ Sew Designs, Disk Part #756 103600, multiformat CD-ROM

Coffee Shop, EZ Sew Designs, Disk Part #756 101400, multiformat CD-ROM

About the Author

M'Liss Rae Hawley is an accomplished quilting teacher, lecturer, embroidery and textile designer, and best-selling author. She conducts workshops and seminars throughout the world. As the author of nine books, including *Phenomenal Fat Quarter Quilts* (2004), *Get Creative! With M'Liss Rae Hawley* (2005), *M'Liss Rae Hawley's Round Robin Renaissance* (2006), and *Mariner's Medallion Quilts* (2006), and the originator of numerous innovative designs, M'Liss is constantly seeking new boundaries to challenge her students while imparting her enthusiasm and love for the art of quilting.

Although her new PBS television series, *M'Liss's Quilting World*, is in production, M'Liss continues to create fabric with coordinating embroidery collections, write books, and contribute to various magazines. She likes to break quilting down to the basics to show students that it can be easy and fun at any skill level.

M'Liss and her husband, Michael, live on Whidbey Island, Washington, in a filbert orchard. Michael is also a best-selling author and the sheriff of Island County. Their son is a sergeant in the Marine Corps, and their daughter, a recent graduate of Seattle University, is serving in AmeriCorps. Michael and M'Liss share their home with five dachshunds, two cats, and two kittens.

Bring Color and Creativity into Your Life

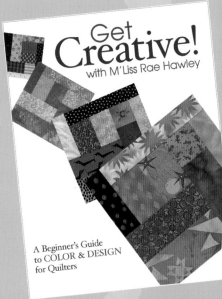

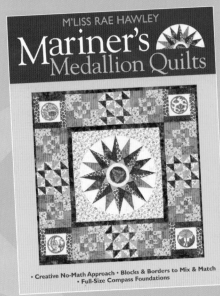